AFRICAN COO

ETHIOPIA • NIGERIA • KENYA

I am a little pencil in the hand of a writing God who is sending a love letter to the world. -Mother Teresa

The world is facing a hunger crisis unlike anything it has seen in more than 50 years.
Every day, almost 16,000 children die from hunger-related causes.
That's one child every five seconds.
In 2010, 7.6 million children died worldwide before their 5th birthday.

There are 84 million inhabitants in Ethiopia.

Per capita income in Ethiopia averages $390 USD per year.
58 percent of Ethiopia's rural population does not have access to clean drinking water.

Ethiopia's poverty-stricken economy is based on agriculture,
accounting for almost 45% of GDP and 85% of total employment.
The agricultural sector suffers from frequent drought and poor cultivation practices.
Coffee is critical to the Ethiopian economy with exports of some $350 million in 2006.

Under Ethiopia's constitution, the state owns all land and provides long-term leases to the tenants.
The system continues to hamper growth in the industrial sector,
as entrepreneurs are unable to use land as collateral for loans.

Ethiopia is also a country with many stories of talents, style and distinction.
In this section we share some of that brilliance as it pertains to
the unique traditions and outstanding flavours of Ethiopian Cuisine.
Join us as we celebrate the cuisine of Ethiopia!

Every action in our lives touches on some chord that will vibrate in eternity. -Edwin Hubbel Chapin

THE COUNTRY OF ETHIOPIA

Ethiopia is a place of high plateaus and low-lying plains.
This ancient country is called the land of thirteen months of sunshine, as the Ethiopian calendar has twelve months
of thirty days, and an extra month of five days called Pagume.
The climate is balmy and pleasant with rain falling rarely except in the summer months.

Primitive and modern cultures exist side by side in Ethiopia.
In the villages, families live in Tukels made of stone with thatched roofs,
and life goes on today much as it has for centuries.
In Addis Ababa, there are new white buildings of reinforced concrete in the midst of bustling, energetic people.
Women with exquisite facial bone structure wear Shamas, a gauzelike white fabric covering them from head to foot.
Men wear either Ethiopian robes or Western attire.

The open-air market of Addis, Ethiopia is the largest and most exciting in all of Africa.
The market seems to stretch for miles.
Everything is on display, from clothing and household wares to treadle sewing machines. For the food at these
markets, women sit cross-legged on the ground with tiny scales to measure spices for the Wat. Grains, called Tef, in
huge bags are ready for the housewives who make Injera bread.
The low stands are heaped with citrus fruits, bananas, grapes, pomegranates, figs, custard apples which are a
delectable tropical fruit, as well as vegetables of all kinds, including the wonderful red onion of this area.
The meats on sale are beef, lamb, and goat. You'll find lab, the soft cheese wrapped and kept cool in banana leaves.

ETHIOPIAN CUISINE

Ethiopian food is a spicy mix of vegetable and lentil stews and slow-simmered meats.
The hottest, most peppery food in all of Africa is found in Ethiopia.
While most Ethiopian cuisine is indigenous, over time ingredients such as red chillies, ginger, and spices
have enriched its flavours.
Grains like millet, sorghum, wheat and ancient Teff form the basic breadstuffs of the diet.

Essential components of Ethiopian cooking are Injera bread, Berbere, a red pepper spice
and Niter Kibbeh, a spice-infused clarified butter.
Most foods have a stewy consistency. Alichas are mild stews. Wats are stews with the spicy flavour of Berbere.
Desserts are not really served in Ethiopia, but Iab, similar to a mixture of cottage cheese and yogurt,
is traditionally the final course of a meal.

Dietary restrictions in religions have given rise to a wide variety of both meat and vegetarian dishes.
There are fast days when meat is prohibited and lentils, peas, and chick peas are used in making the Wat and Alicha.
No one is permitted to eat pork.

Most farming in Ethiopia is subsistence, so the vegetables and animals are often grown and raised at home.
Ethiopia has been called the "Land of Bread and Honey".
The ancient practice of beekeeping produces exquisite honey.
Honey is fermented to Tej, a honey wine.

SERVING DINNER IN ETHIOPIA

A meal in Ethiopia is an experience!
The guests are seated round the table on stools about eight inches high
and a Mesab, a handmade wicker hourglass-shaped table and a designed domed cover is set before them.

A tall, stunning woman with characteristically high cheekbones and soft skin, dressed in a Shama,
carries a long-spouted copper pitcher in her right hand, a copper basin in her left hand, and a towel over her left arm.
She pours warm water over the fingers of your right hand, holding the basin to catch the excess, and you wipe your hands on the towel that hangs over her arm.

The meal is then served on a large platter that is draped with crepe-like Injera bread.
All guests eat from this one platter.
Various dishes are brought to the table in enamel bowls and portioned out onto the Injera.
Guests simply tear off a piece of the bread, use it to scoop up some of the various stews and pop it in their mouths.

The server then returns with individual long-necked bottles from which you drink Tej, an amber-coloured honey wine which is put on a little table close by.
She may also serve beverages such as weakly carbonated water or Telba, a flaxseed drink.
Another hand washing ends the meal and strong coffee is served on a tray in tiny Japanese cups served black with sugar.
Frankincense is then burned.

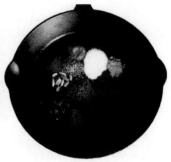

STAPLE ITEMS

Two essential components of Ethiopian cooking are Berbere, peppery spice,
and Niter Kibbeh, spiced clarified butter.
Berbere, along with Niter Kibbeh, supplies one of the unique flavours of Ethiopian cuisine.
These two items are frequently used and are the perfect place to begin your Ethiopian Cooking.

Essential spices in Ethiopian cooking are; fenugreek seeds, crushed mustard seeds, crushed caraway seeds,
cardamom seeds, cardamom pods, whole cumin, whole peppercorns, whole cloves,
allspice berries, dried chillies, red pepper flakes,
paprika, salt, pepper, turmeric, cayenne pepper,
nutmeg, cinnamon,
gingerroot, ground ginger, crushed garlic,
basil, oregano, parsley and coriander.

The most commonly used vegetables are; onions, carrots, green peas, lentils, tomatoes, potatoes,
lemons, cabbage, sweet potatoes, cucumbers and corn.

Important cooking utensils are; spice grinder, large cast iron skillet, frying pan, food processor or blender and if
possible an Injera platter.

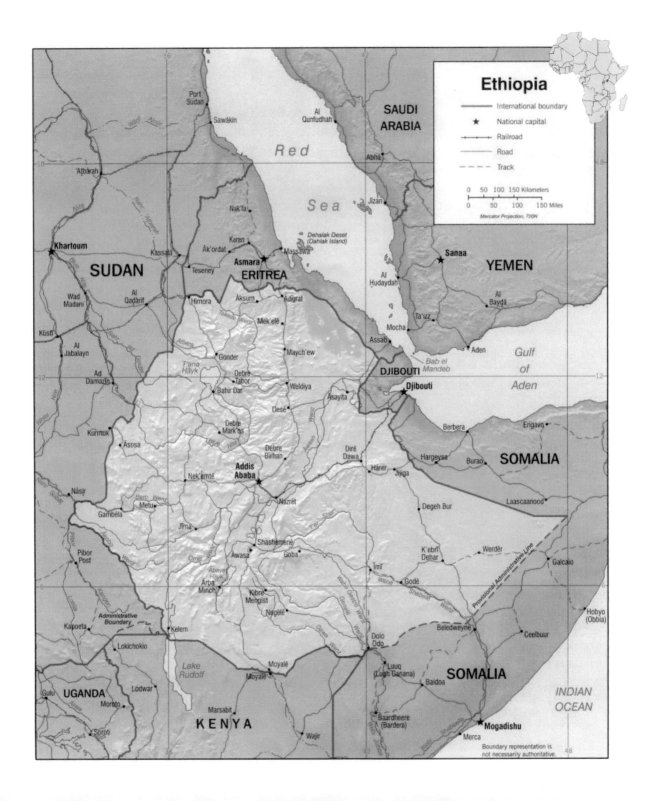

Ethiopia

- ———— International boundary
- ★ National capital
- ┼┼┼ Railroad
- ——— Road
- – – – Track

0 50 100 150 Kilometers
0   50   100   150 Miles

Mercator Projection, 72ºN

SAUDI ARABIA

Port Sudan
Sawâkin
Al Qunfudhah
Abhá

Red

Sea

Jizan

'Atbârah

Nak'fa

Dehalak Deset
(Dahlak Island)

Sanaa

YEMEN

Khartoum
Kassala
Äk'ordat
Keren
Massawa
Asmara
ERITREA

SUDAN

Teseney

Al Hudaydah
Al Baydá
Ta'izz

Wad Madani
Al Qadarif
Himora
Aksum
Adigrat
Mek'elé

Mocha
Assab
Aden

Gulf
of
Aden

Küsti
Al Jabalayn

Maych'ew

Gonder

Bab el Mandeb

DJIBOUTI
Djibouti

Ad Damazin

T'ana Hâyk
Debre Tabor
Bahir Dar
Weldiya
Desé
Åsayita

Berbera
Erigavo

Kurmuk

Åsosa

Debre Mark'os

Debre Birhan

Diré Dawa
Hárer
Jijiga

Hargeysa
Burao
SOMALIA

Nâsir

Addis Ababa
Nek'emte

Nazrét

Degeh Bur

Laascaanood

Gambêla
Metu

Jima

Shashemenê

K'ebri Dehar
Werdèr

Galcaio

Awasa
Goba

Îmî
Godé

Pibor Post

Åbeyet Hâyk
Arba Minch

Kibre Mengist

Negélé

Hobyo (Obbia)

Administrative Boundary

Kapoeta
Kelem

Dolo Odo

Beledweyne
Ceelbuur

Lokichokio

Moyalé
Moyalé

Luuq (Lugh Ganana)

Baidoa

SOMALIA

Lake Rudolf

UGANDA

Gulu
Lödwar

Moroto

Marsabit

Baardheere (Bardera)

Wajir

KENYA

★ **Mogadishu**
Merca

INDIAN OCEAN

Provisional Administrative Line

Boundary representation is not necessarily authoritative.

INDEX

1 - Red Pepper Spice
Berbere

Description: *Berbere* is a red pepper spice mixture and a key ingredient in Ethiopian cuisine.

Preparation Time: 5 minutes
Cooking Time: 2 minutes
Serving Size: 1/3 cup

Ingredients:

Whole cumin	2 tsp
Red pepper flakes	1 tsp
Cardamom seeds	1 tsp
Fenugreek seeds	1 tsp
Whole peppercorns	8
Allspice berries	6
Whole cloves	4
Paprika	1 tbsp
Salt	1 tbsp
Ground ginger	1 tsp
Turmeric	1 tsp
Cayenne pepper	1 tsp
Nutmeg	1/2 tsp

Method:

1. Heat a cast-iron skillet over medium flame. Add the whole spices and toast, stirring for 2 to 3 minutes until they give off their aroma. Do not burn. Remove from heat.
2. Put the spices into a spice or coffee grinder and grind to a powder.

For Variation:

1. You can make Berbere as spicy or as mild as you like by varying the amount of pepper flakes and cayenne pepper.

2 - Spiced Clarified Butter

Niter Kibbeh

Description: *Niter kibbeh* is a spiced, clarified butter and a very important cooking medium in Ethiopian cuisine. It adds an incomparable flavour to dishes. Plain butter or oil can be substituted in Ethiopian recipes if you don't have the time to make *niter kibbeh*, but something special will be missing.

Preparation Time: 5 minutes
Cooking Time: 1 hour
Serving Size: 2 cups

Ingredients:

Unsalted butter	1 lb
Onion (chopped)	1 cup
Garlic (crushed)	2-3 cloves
Gingerroot (cut in ¼ inch slices)	2-3 pieces
Cardamom pods	3-4
Ground cinnamon	1 tsp
Whole cloves	3-4
Fenugreek seeds	1 tsp
Turmeric	1/2 tsp

Method:

1. Place the butter in a small saucepan and melt over low heat.
2. Add the remaining ingredients and simmer on the lowest possible heat for about 1 hour.
3. Pour the clear golden liquid off the top leaving all the solids in the bottom of the pan. Strain if necessary. Discard solids.
4. Store in the refrigerator or freezer and use as needed.

3 - Onion Wat

Sum Sikil

Preparation Time: 20 minutes
Cooking Time: 30 minutes
Serving Size: 6

Ingredients:

Red onions (chopped)	6 cups
Garlic (chopped)	3 tbsp
Olive oil	1 cup
Green chilli paste	1 tbsp
Salt	1 tbsp
Curry powder	1 tbsp
Ground cardamom	1 tbsp
Ground cloves	1 tsp
Oregano	1 tsp
Sweet basil	1 tsp
Ground cinnamon	1 tsp
Tomato paste	1 ½ cups

Method:

1. Chop onions and garlic. Put them into a covered casserole dish, without oil or water. At high heat, stir constantly until the onions appear cooked.
2. Add one cup of olive oil. Lower heat to medium, and simmer uncovered for 10 minutes.
3. Add green chilli paste and stir until completely blended.
4. Stirring all the while, add salt, curry powder, ground cardamom, ground cloves, oregano, sweet basil and ground cinnamon.
5. Reduce heat to low and simmer 10 minutes.
6. If desired, add tomato paste and stir until completely blended.
7. Simmer for an additional 10 minutes.

4 - Vegetable Wat

Yatakelt

Preparation Time: 5 minutes
Cooking Time: 30 minutes
Serving Size: 6

Ingredients:

Red onions (finely chopped)	1 cup
Garlic (minced)	2 cloves
Berbere	1 tsp
Paprika	1 tsp
Niter kibbeh	1/4 cup
Green beans (cut in thirds)	1 cup
Carrots (chopped)	1 cup
Potatoes (cubed)	1 cup
Tomatoes (chopped)	1 cup
Tomato paste	1/4 cup
Vegetable stock	2 cups
Salt	to taste
Black pepper	to taste
Fresh parsley (chopped)	1/4 cup
Injera	2 batches
Plain yogurt or cottage cheese	

Method:

1. Sauté the onions, garlic, berbere and paprika in the niter kibbeh for 2 minutes.
2. Add the beans, carrots, and potatoes. Continue to sauté for 10 minutes, stirring occasionally to prevent burning.
3. Add the chopped tomatoes, tomato paste and the vegetable stock.
4. Bring to a boil and then simmer for 15 minutes, or until all of the vegetables are tender.
5. Add salt and pepper to taste and mix in the parsley.
6. Serve with Injera and yogurt or cottage cheese.

5 - Chickpea Wat

Yeshiro

Preparation Time: 15 minutes
Cooking Time: 45 minutes
Serving Size: 6

Ingredients:

Olive oil	2 tbsp
Red onion (finely chopped)	1
Carrots (finely chopped)	2
Potato (peeled, chopped)	1
Cayenne pepper	1/2 tsp
Paprika	1/2 tsp
Ground ginger	1/2 tsp
Salt	1/2 tsp
Black pepper	1/2 tsp
Cumin	1/4 tsp
Cardamom	1/4 tsp
Tomato paste	1 tbsp
Chickpeas (drained, rinsed)	1 cup
Water	1 ½ cups
Peas	1 cup

Method:

1. Heat the oil in a large pot over medium heat. Add the onion, cover and cook for 5 minutes until softened.
2. Add the carrots and potato, cover and cook 10 minutes longer.
3. Remove and cover and stir in cayenne, paprika, ginger, salt, pepper, cumin, cardamom and tomato paste.
4. Add chickpeas and water and bring to a boil. Reduce heat to low and simmer for 20 minutes, covered.
5. Stir in green peas and taste to adjust seasonings. Simmer for 10 more minutes until vegetables are tender and the flavour is developed. Add a bit more water if needed.

6 - Lentil Wat

Yemesir

Preparation Time: 5 minutes
Cooking Time: 1 hour
Serving Size: 4 to 6

Ingredients:

Onions (chopped)	2 cups
Garlic (crushed)	2 cloves
Ginger (peeled, minced)	2 tsp
Oil, butter or niter kibbeh	1/4 cup
Turmeric	1 tsp
Paprika	2 tbsp
Cayenne pepper	1/2 to 2 tsp
Red lentils (rinsed)	2 cups
Water or stock	4 cups
Salt	to taste
Black pepper	to taste

Method:

1.Place the onion, garlic and ginger in a food processor or blender and puree. Add a little water if necessary.
2.Heat the oil, butter or niter kibbeh in a large, heavy-bottomed saucepan over medium heat.
3.Add turmeric, paprika and cayenne pepper. Stir rapidly for 30 seconds to color the oil and cook spices through.
4.Add the onion puree and sauté for 5 to 20 minutes, until the excess moisture evaporates and the onion loses its raw aroma.
5.Add lentils and water to the saucepan. Bring to a boil, reduce heat to low, and simmer for 30 to 40 minutes until lentils are cooked through and fall apart. Add water if necessary to keep the lentils from drying out.
6.Stir in salt and pepper to taste.

For Variation:

1.To make *Shiro Wat*; use split green peas instead of lentils.
2.Substitute yellow lentils if you prefer.

7 - Chicken, Zucchini or Lamb Wat

Doro, Sik Sik, Sega

Preparation Time: 40 minutes
Cooking Time: 45 minutes
Serving Size: 4 to 6

Ingredients:

Skinless chicken legs and thighs	2 lbs
Lemon (juice)	1
Salt	2 tsp
Onions (chopped)	2
Garlic (crushed)	2 tbsp
Gingerroot (peeled, chopped)	1 tbsp
Oil, butter or niter kibbeh	1/4 cup
Paprika	2 tbsp
Berbere	2 tsp
Water or stock	3/4 cup
Red wine	1/3 cup
Cayenne pepper	from 1 tsp
Salt	to taste
Black pepper	to taste
Hard boiled eggs	4

Method:

1. Mix together the chicken pieces, lemon juice and salt in a large, non-reactive bowl and set aside to marinate for 30 minutes.
2. While the chicken is marinating, puree the onions, garlic and ginger in a food processor or blender. Add a little water if necessary.
3. Heat the oil, butter or niter kibbeh in a large pot over medium flame. Add the paprika and stir for 1 minute to color the oil and cook the spice through. Do not burn. Stir in the berbere paste and cook for another 2 to 3 minutes.
4. Add the onion-garlic-ginger puree and sauté for 5 to 10 minutes until most of the moisture evaporates and the onion cooks down and loses its raw aroma. Do not allow the mixture to burn.
5. Pour in the water or stock and wine. Stir in the chicken pieces (without the marinade), cayenne, salt and pepper to taste. Bring to a boil, reduce heat to low, cover and simmer for 45 minutes. Add water as necessary to maintain a sauce-like consistency.
6. Add the whole hard boiled eggs and continue to cook for another 10 to 15 minutes, or until the chicken is cooked through and very tender.
7. Adjust seasoning and serve hot with Injera or rice.

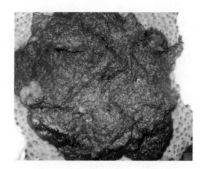

For Variation:
1. *Chicken Wat* is traditionally very spicy, but you can adjust the amount of cayenne pepper to your liking.

2. To make *Sik Sik Wat,* substitute 2 lbs of small zucchini, halved and quartered. Proceed with the recipe, but just cook long enough for the zucchini to be cooked through and soft.

3. To make *Sega Wat*, substitute 2 lbs of lamb for the chicken in this recipe.

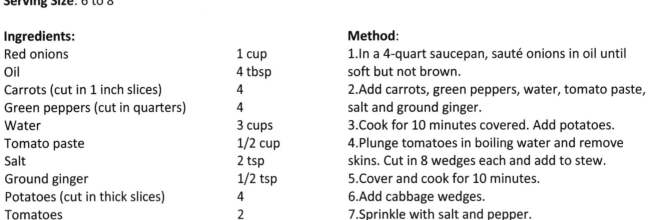

8 - Vegetable Alicha

Yatakelt

Preparation Time: 10 minutes
Cooking Time: 25 minutes
Serving Size: 6 to 8

Ingredients:

Red onions	1 cup
Oil	4 tbsp
Carrots (cut in 1 inch slices)	4
Green peppers (cut in quarters)	4
Water	3 cups
Tomato paste	1/2 cup
Salt	2 tsp
Ground ginger	1/2 tsp
Potatoes (cut in thick slices)	4
Tomatoes	2
Cabbage wedges (cut in 1 inch cubes)	8
Salt	to taste
Black pepper	to taste

Method:

1. In a 4-quart saucepan, sauté onions in oil until soft but not brown.
2. Add carrots, green peppers, water, tomato paste, salt and ground ginger.
3. Cook for 10 minutes covered. Add potatoes.
4. Plunge tomatoes in boiling water and remove skins. Cut in 8 wedges each and add to stew.
5. Cover and cook for 10 minutes.
6. Add cabbage wedges.
7. Sprinkle with salt and pepper.
8. Cook until vegetables are tender.
9. Correct the seasoning.

9 - Chicken Alicha

Doro

Preparation Time: 10 minutes
Cooking Time: 55 minutes
Serving Size: 4

Ingredients:

Chicken (cut in parts, without skin)	1 lb
Lime (juice)	1
Red onions	6 cups
Niter kibbeh	2 cups
Red wine	1/2 cup
Black pepper	1/4 tsp
Garlic powder	1/4 tsp
Ground ginger	1/4 tsp
Salt	to taste
Water	4 cups
Hard-boiled eggs	4

Method:

1. Wash the chicken parts and soak in water with lime juice.
2. In a large pot, fry the onions until tender. Add niter kibbeh and stir. Add ½ cup of water and the wine. Add spices.
3. Add the chicken.
4. Add more water if necessary, and cook for 45 minutes until the sauce is reduced.
5. Add eggs (if desired) and serve.

10 - Beef or Lamb Alicha

Saga, Sega

Preparation Time: 15 minutes
Cooking Time: 1 hour
Serving Size: 6

Ingredients:

Red onion (sliced)	1 cup
Corn oil	2 tbsp
Beef or lamb	2 lbs
Garlic cloves (sliced)	2
Salt	1 tsp
Hot green chilli pepper (sliced)	1
Gingerroot (crushed)	1/4 tsp
Mustard seeds (crushed)	1/4 tsp
Caraway seed (crushed)	1/4 tsp
Ground turmeric	1/4 tsp
Water	1/2 cups

Method:

1.In dry pan over medium heat, stir-fry onions for 2 minutes.

2.Add the oil and stir-fry 1 minute longer. Add the meat and brown 5 minutes, stirring frequently.

3.Add all of the spices and seasonings at one time and stir well.

4.Add the water and bring to a boil. Cover the pan and cook over low heat for 45 minutes, or until the meat is tender.

5.Should the curry dry out too quickly, add another ½ cup water.

6.At the end of the 45 minutes, there should be very little sauce.

7.Serve warm or at room temperature.

11 - Vegetable Stew
Yetakelt

Preparation Time: 15 minutes
Cooking Time: 40 minutes
Serving Size: 4 to 6

Ingredients:

Oil	4 tbsp
Onions (chopped)	1 cup
Berbere	3 tsp
Carrots (cut in 1 inch slices)	3
Green bell peppers (quartered)	3
Water	3 cups
Tomato sauce	3/4 cups
Salt	2 tsp
Ground ginger	1/2 tsp
Potatoes (cut in thick slices)	4
Tomatoes (skinned, cut in wedges)	2
Cabbage (cut in 1 inch wedges)	8
Black pepper	to taste

Method:

1.Add the oil and onions to a large saucepan and fry on medium for 5 minutes or until the onions have softened.

2.Add berbere and fry for one minute.

3.Add carrots, green peppers, water, tomato sauce, salt and ground ginger. Bring to a simmer and cook for 10 minutes.

4.Add potatoes and tomatoes. Cover and cook for 10 minutes.

5.Add cabbage. Season to taste and cook for 25 minutes or until the vegetables are completely tender.

12 - Beef Stew

Saga

Preparation Time: 30 minutes
Cooking Time: 1 hour
Serving Size: 8

Ingredients:

Butter or niter kibbeh	½ cup
Red onions (chopped finely)	3
Chilli paste	1/4 cup
Canned crushed tomatoes	1 cup
Beef brisket (cut in 1/2 inch cubes)	2 lbs

Method:

1. Heat a pan (3 to 4 inches deep).
2. Add half of the butter or niter kibbeh.
3. Once butter is melted, add the onions and cook it until the onions are caramelized.
4. Add chilli paste to the cooked onions. Cook for 15 minutes, stirring often and adding a drop of water as needed to prevent it from drying out.
5. Add tomatoes and cook for 30 minutes more, stirring it often and adding a drop of water as needed to prevent it from drying out.
6. Add beef to the cooking paste and cook covered for 25 minutes or until cooked fully.

13 - Sautéed Lamb or Beef

Gomen Sega

Preparation Time: 5 minutes
Cooking Time: 15 minutes
Serving Size: 4 to 6

Ingredients:

Lean lamb or beef (cut in long strips)	1 lb
Garlic clove	1
Olive oil	1 tbsp
Sweet onion (thinly sliced)	1
Green hot peppers (thinly sliced)	3
Red bell pepper (thinly sliced)	1
Salt	a pinch
Butter	1 tbsp
Berbere spice	3-4 tbsp

Method:

1. Mix meat with garlic.
2. Heat oil over medium-high heat.
3. Saute onion and hot peppers for 5 minutes, or until onion is light golden.
5. Add red bell pepper and salt. Sauté 2 to 3 minutes until red pepper is tender.
6. Transfer onion mixture to a bowl.
7. In same pan, melt butter over high heat and sauté meat mixture for 2 minutes.
8. Stir in berbere spice mix to taste. Sauté for 30 seconds.
9. Serve with Injera or Tomato and Cucumber salad.

14 - Lamb

Sega

Preparation Time: 10 minutes
Cooking Time: 1 hour
Serving Size: 6

Ingredients:

Mustard greens (chopped)	4 lbs
Beef (diced)	2 lbs
Red onion (chopped)	1
Medium green pepper (chopped)	2
Salt	to taste
Black pepper	to taste
Niter kibbeh	6 tbsp
Medium scallion (chopped)	8
Medium serrano pepper (chopped)	4

Method:

1. Place mustard greens in a large pot and simmer for 10 minutes. Do not add water. Enough water clings to the greens in the cleaning process.
2. Drain and set aside.
3. In Dutch oven, sauté beef, onion, green pepper, salt and pepper until beef is brown.
4. Add mustard greens and remaining ingredients.
5. Cook for 1 hour or until liquid in pan has evaporated.

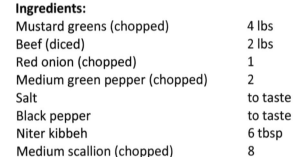

15 - Mashed Potatoes

Solanum Tubersum

Preparation Time: 15 minutes
Cooking Time: 25 minutes
Serving Size: 6

Ingredients:

Potatoes (diced)	2 ¼ cups
Sweet potatoes (diced)	1 ¾ cups
Whole kernel corn	1 cup
Light coconut milk	3/4 cup
Olive oil	1 tbsp
Butter	1 tbsp
Curry powder	1 tsp
Salt	1/2 tsp
Turmeric	1/4 tsp

Method:

1.Place potatoes and sweet potatoes in a saucepan. Cover with water and bring to a boil.
2.Reduce heat and simmer for 10 minutes, or until potatoes are almost tender.
3.Add corn to pan and cook 5 minutes, or until potatoes are tender.
4.Drain well. Place potato mixture in a large bowl, and mash potato mixture with a potato masher.
5.Combine coconut milk, oil, and butter in a small saucepan. Bring to a boil.
6.Stir milk mixture, curry, salt and turmeric into potato mixture.

16 - Hot and Spicy African Wraps

Doro

Preparation Time: 30 minutes
Cooking Time: 3 hours and 20 minutes
Serving Size: 4

Ingredients:

Chicken thigh fillet	2 lbs
Lemon (juice)	1
Salt	1/2 tbsp
Onion	1
Garlic cloves	2
Olive oil	1 tbsp
Berbere	2 tsp
Ginger (minced)	1 tbsp
Nutmeg	a pinch
Ground cardamom	a pinch
Red wine	1/4 cup
Chicken stock	2 cups
Tomato paste	1/2 cup
Coriander (chopped)	1 cup
Kita	4
Butter	2 tbsp

Method:

1. Place chicken in dish and cover with lemon juice and salt. Marinate in fridge for 30 minutes.
2. Chop onion and garlic. Cook in a large heavy pot with the olive oil until soft.
3. Add berbere mix, ginger, nutmeg, cardamom and stir-fry for 1 minute.
4. Add wine, stock and tomato paste and bring to simmer.
5. Add chicken and marinade mixture. Bring to boil, then reduce to simmer.
6. Simmer at very low temperature with lid on for 3 hours, stirring frequently and ensuring stew doesn't dry out or stick to bottom.
7. Add coriander.
8. Melt butter in frying pan. Cook Kita quickly turning so they puff up.
9. Fill Kita with stew and wrap.

17 - Flatbread

Injera

Preparation Time: 5 minutes
Cooking Time: 25 minutes
Serving Size: 6 to 8 Crepes

Ingredients:

Teff Flour	1 ½ cups
Water	2 cups
Salt	1/2 tsp
Vegetable oil	
Lemon (juice)	1

Method:

1.Mix the teff flour with the water. Cover with a towel and let stand at room temperature until it bubbles and has fermented. The consistency should be comparable to a very thin pancake batter. This process may take up to 3 days. Each morning, gently disturb the mixture with a wooden spoon. There should be bubbles forming on the surface, it should smell sour and water should have risen to the top. If not yet ready, cover again and let stand again overnight.

2.Gradually stir in the salt until well mixed.

3.Preheat a large cast-iron skillet over a medium heat.

4.Wipe the skillet with a little oil using a paper towel.

5.Ladle about 1/2 cup of batter to cover the bottom of the skillet. Spread the batter around immediately with a spatula to make a large crepe.

6.Let bake in the skillet about 2 to 3 minutes, until holes form in the Injera and the edges begin to dry out.

7.Carefully turn the Injera over and cook on second side for 1 to 2 minutes. Try to not brown too much. Remove the Injera to a platter to cool.

8.Repeat with the rest of the batter, wiping the skillet clean with an oiled paper towel each time. Place plastic or foil between Injera so that they do not stick.

9.After the batter is used up, brush each Injera with the lemon juice.

10.Serve immediately or keep covered in a warm oven.

18 - Unleavened Flatbread

Kita

Preparation Time: 7 minutes
Cooking Time: 10 minutes
Serving Size: 12 to 14 Crepes

Ingredients:

Ingredient	Amount
All purpose flour	1 cup
Whole wheat flour	1 cup
Oil	1/2 cup
Salt	1 tsp
Water	1 cup

Method:

1.Heat oil in cast-iron skillet.
2.Mix flours and salt together in a bowl and salt. Gradually add the heated oil.
3.Gradually add up to 1 cup of lukewarm water while kneading to make dough.
4. Spread flour on a flat clean surface and form bun sized dough.
5.Roll out the dough with a rolling pin on the floured board until very thin and roughly in a round shape.
6.Cook in the cast-iron skillet until slightly puffed and brown.

Variations:

1.You can deep fry the Kita in oil if you would like to have them puff up.
2.Depending on what you are serving, you can spice with sage, thyme and summer savoury.

19 - Spiced Honey Bread

Yemarin Yewotet Dabo

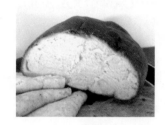

Preparation Time: 2 hours
Cooking Time: 1 hour
Serving Size: 1 loaf

Ingredients:

Active dry yeast	1/4 oz
Lukewarm water	1/4 cup
Egg (beaten)	1
Honey	1/2 cup
Ground coriander	1 tbsp
Ground cinnamon	1 tsp
Ground cloves	1/2 tsp
Salt	1 tsp
Warm milk	1 cup
Butter (melted)	6 tbsp
Flour	4-5 cups

Method:

1.Preheat oven to 325°F.
2.In a small bowl, stir together the yeast and 1/4 cup warm water. Set for about 10 minutes.
3.In a large bowl, beat together the egg, honey, spices and salt until smooth. Stir in the milk and melted butter.

4.Stir in the flour, 1/2 cup at a time, mixing to form a soft, smooth dough. Do not add all of the flour if the dough gets too stiff. Add more flour if the dough gets too sticky.
5.Remove the dough to a lightly floured work surface and knead for 10 minutes to form a smooth, elastic dough.
6.Place the dough in a large, lightly oiled bowl, cover with plastic wrap and let rise in a warm place until doubled in size, about 1 ½ hours.
7.Remove the dough again to a lightly floured work surface and punch down the dough. Knead for 1 minute. Form the dough into a round and place on an oiled baking sheet. Allow to rise again another 30 to 45 minutes.
8.Place bread on baking sheet in the oven and bake 45 minutes to 1 hour until bread is lightly browned and sounds hollow.

20 - Fried Turnover

Sambusa

Preparation Time: 20 minutes
Cooking Time: 30 minutes
Serving Size: 48

Ingredients:

Ingredient	Amount
Red onion (finely chopped)	1/2 cup
Lean ground lamb or beef (browned)	1 lb
Ginger (minced)	1/2 tsp
Ground turmeric	1/2 tsp
Garlic (minced)	1/2 tsp
Cayenne pepper	1/2 tsp
Salt	to taste
Cinnamon	1/2 tsp
Coriander sprigs (chopped)	4
Mint sprigs (chopped)	3
Water	2 cups
Wonton wrappers	48

Method:

1. Combine all ingredients (except for wonton wrappers) in a heavy saucepan.
2. Bring to a boil and stir to keep smooth.
3. Reduce heat to medium and let mixture simmer uncovered.
4. Correct flavour for spices and salt.
5. As water simmers away, stir often to prevent mixture from sticking, especially during final stages.
6. Cook until all liquid evaporates.
7. If ground meat has a lot of fat, drain off at this point.
8. Let mixture cool slightly before stuffing.
9. Fill wonton wrappers with 1 to 2 tsp of filling. Moisten and press the edges together in a triangle shape.
10. Fry the Sambusas, several at a time, until golden brown on both sides. Place the golden brown Sambusas on paper towel to rid of excess oil.
11. Serve hot or cold and with or without chutney.

21 - Lentil Soup

Yemiser

Preparation Time: 10 minutes
Cooking Time: 20 minutes
Serving Size: 8

Ingredients:

Dried brown or rinsed canned lentils	1 cup
Onion (finely chopped)	1 cup
Garlic (minced)	2 cloves
Niter kibbeh	1/4 cup
Berbere	1 tsp
Ground cumin seeds	1 tsp
Paprika	1 tsp
Tomato (finely chopped)	2 cups
Tomato paste	1/2 cup
Vegetable stock or water	1 cup
Green peas	1 cup
Salt	to taste
Black pepper	to taste

Method:

1. Rinse and cook the lentils.
2. Meanwhile sauté the onions and garlic in the niter kibbeh until the onions are translucent.
3. Add the berbere, cumin and paprika. Sauté for a few minutes more, stirring occasionally to prevent burning.
4. Mix in the chopped tomatoes and tomato paste. Simmer for another 5 to 10 minutes.
5. Add vegetable stock or water and continue simmering.
6. When the lentils are cooked, drain and mix them into the sauté mixture.
7. Add the green peas and cook for another 5 minutes. Add salt and pepper to taste.

22 - Spicy Lentil Salad

Azifa

Preparation Time: 10 minutes
Cooking Time: 30 minutes
Serving Size: 4

Ingredients:

Lentils	1/2 lb
Garlic (crushed)	1/4 tsp
Red onion	1/2 cup
Canned green chillies (chopped)	1/4 cup
Chillies (thinly sliced)	3
Fresh basil (chopped)	3 tbsp
Fresh parsley	1/2 tsp
Lemon (juice)	2 tsp
Salt	1/4 tsp
Balsamic vinegar	1 tsp
Olive oil	3 tbsp
Diced tomato for garnish	1

Method:

1. Cook lentils.
2. Drain, rinse and place lentils in a bowl.
3. Combine lentils with all remaining ingredients (except tomato). Toss gently.
4. Place in refrigerator.
5. Stir occasionally while salad is chilling.
6. Add tomato as garnish and serve.

23 - Tomato and Cucumber Salad
Quia

Preparation Time: 15 minutes
Cooking Time: 0 minutes
Serving Size: 4

Ingredients:

Ingredient	Amount
Tomatoes (seeded, diced)	2 cups
Cucumbers (diced)	1 ½ cups
Sweet onion (diced)	1/4 cup
Green hot pepper (seeded, diced)	1
Lemon (juice)	4 tsp
Balsamic vinegar	2 tsp
Salt	1/4 tsp
Black pepper	1/4 tsp
Olive oil	2 tsp

Method:
1. Toss together all ingredients.
2. Sprinkle with olive oil.

24 - Hot Cabbage Salad

Tikil Gomen

Preparation Time: 10 minutes
Cooking Time: 45 minutes
Serving Size: 4 to 6

Ingredients:

Olive oil	3-4 tbsp
Carrots (thinly sliced)	4
Onion (thinly sliced)	1
Salt	1 tsp
Black pepper	1/2 tsp
Cumin	1/2 tsp
Turmeric	1/4 tsp
Cabbage (shredded)	1/2 head
Potatoes (cut in 1 inch cubes)	5

Method:

1. Heat the olive over medium heat in a medium skillet.
2. Add the carrots and onion. Cook in the hot oil for 5 minutes.
3. Add the salt, pepper, cumin, turmeric and cabbage. Cook 15 to 20 minutes.
4. Stir in the potatoes. Cover and reduce heat to low. Cook 15 to 20 minutes, or until potatoes are soft.

25 - Little Fried Snacks

Dabo Kolo

Preparation Time: 15 minutes
Cooking Time: 15 minutes
Serving Size: 6 to 8

Ingredients:

All purpose flour	2 cups
Salt	1/2 tsp
Sugar	2 tbsp
Cayenne pepper	1/2 tsp
Oil	1/4 cup
Water	

Method:

1.In a 1-quart bowl mix flour, salt, sugar, cayenne pepper and oil.
2.Knead together and add water spoonful by spoonful to form stiff dough.
3.Knead dough for 5 more minutes.
4.Tear off a piece the size of a golf ball.
5.Roll it out with palms of hands on a lightly floured board into a long strip 1/2 inch thick.
6.Snip into 1/2 inch pieces with scissors.
7.Spread about a handful of the pieces on an ungreased 9 inch frying pan. Cook over heat until uniformly light brown on all sides, stirring up once in a while as you go along.
8.Continue until all are light brown. Serve as a snack.

26 - Fresh Cheese

lab

Description: *lab* is a fresh cheese similar to cottage cheese. Its cooling flavour is the perfect addition for many spicy Ethiopian dishes. *lab* is often served as the finish to an Ethiopian meal.

Preparation Time: 3 minutes
Cooking Time: 0 minutes
Serving Size: 2 cups

Ingredients:

Cottage cheese	2 cups
Plain yogurt	1/2 cup
Lemon juice	2 tbsp
Salt	to taste
Black pepper	to taste

Method:

1.Place the cottage cheese, yogurt, lemon juice, salt and pepper into a large bowl and use a wooden spoon to stir together. Lightly mash the cheese curds.

2.Adjust seasoning and serve as a side dish or as the final course to an Ethiopian meal.

For Variation:

1.To make *lab be Gomen* (Fresh Cheese with greens); stir in 2 cups of chopped and sautéed collard greens.

2.For added flavour, you can stir in chopped parsley, spinach or fenugreek leaves.

3.Fresh lemon zest can also be added.

27 - Flaxseed Beverage

Telba

Description: *Telba* is a healthy and refreshingly creamy beverage.

Preparation Time: 25 minutes
Cooking Time: 5 minutes
Serving Size: 4 to 6

Ingredients:

Flaxseed	1 cup
Water	6 cups
Honey	2 tbsp

Method:

1. Heat a cast-iron skillet over low heat.
2. Add the flaxseed and dry roast it in the skillet, stirring for 5 to 10 minutes. Remove from heat and set aside to cool.
3. Place the toasted flaxseed in a spice grinder and grind to a powder. Sift through a medium-mesh sieve into a bowl.
4. Add the water to the flaxseed, stir and let set for 15 minutes to allow solids to settle out.
5. Strain to a pitcher. Add honey and chill before serving.

One man gives freely, yet gains even more; another withholds unduly, but comes to poverty. A generous man will prosper; he who refreshes others will himself be refreshed. -Proverbs 11:24-25

Nigeria is the largest country in Africa with 170 million inhabitants.
Despite Nigeria's plentiful agricultural resources and oil wealth as Africa's second largest economy,
poverty is rising with almost 100 million people living on less than $1 a day.
Over 70 percent of Nigerians are now classified as poor and 35 percent live in absolute poverty.

Poverty is especially severe in rural areas,
where up to 80 percent of the population live below the poverty line,
and social services and infrastructure are limited.

The country's poor rural women and men depend on agriculture for food and income.
About 90 percent of Nigeria's food is produced by small-scale farmers,
who cultivate small plots of land and depend on rainfall rather than irrigation systems.

Although Nigeria's economy is projected to continue growing, poverty is likely to worsen,
as the gap between rich and poor in Africa's largest oil producer continues to widen.
Many communities need access to safe water, agricultural supplies and training,
education, basic medical attention and small business opportunities.
Proceeds from the sale of this book will help bring about change for Nigerian communities.

Nigeria is also a country with many stories of talent and excellence as actors, musicians, artists and professionals.
In this section we share some of that excellence as it pertains to
the unique traditions and outstanding flavours of Nigerian Cuisine.

Each time a man stands up for an ideal, or acts to improve the lot of others, or strikes out against injustice, he sends forth a tiny ripple of hope... daring those ripples to build a current that can sweep down the mightiest walls or oppression and resistance. -Robert F Kennedy

THE COUNTRY OF NIGERIA

Nigeria is a West African country bordering the Gulf of Guinea, between Benin, Cameroon and Niger to the north.
Home to 170 million people, Nigeria is the most populous country in Africa and seventh in the world.
Nigeria spans 574,002 square miles (923,768 square kilometers), which is twice the size of California.
Nigeria borders the Atlantic Ocean with 853 kilometers of coastline.
The name Nigeria is taken from the Niger River, which plays an important role in Nigerian lives
as a transportation highway, an excellent source of fish, as well as providing the water needed to cultivate crops.

Natural resources are natural gas, petroleum, tin, iron ore, coal, limestone, niobium, lead, zinc and arable land.
Nigeria is the world's largest producer of cassava, yam and cowpea, which are staple foods in sub-Saharan Africa.
It is also a major producer of fish,
yet it is a food-deficit nation and imports large amounts of grain, livestock products and fish.

Nigeria's capital city is Abuja, which is located in the heart of Nigeria, about 480 kilometers from Lagos.
Lagos is the largest city in Nigeria with a population of 10.2 million, followed by Kano, Ibadan and Abuja at 2 million.
Nigeria consists of 36 states and the Federal Capital Territory of Abuja,
with approximately 75 percent of Nigeria's populace living in the rural areas.

Nigeria is composed of more than 250 ethnic groups. The following are the most populous:
Hausa and Fulani 29%, Yoruba 21%, Igbo (Ibo) 18%, Ijaw 10%, Kanuri 4%, Ibibio 3.5% and Tiv 2.5%
The official language was chosen to be English to facilitate the cultural and linguistic unity of the country,
however there are over 500 living indigenous languages.

Nigeria's terrain is beautiful with the southern lowlands merging into central hills and plateaus,
the mountain range in the southeast and plains in the north.
The main rivers are the Niger and the Benue River which converge and empty into the Niger Delta.

The climate varies from equatorial in the south, to tropical in the center and arid in the north.
The country experiences consistently high temperatures all year round,
therefore rainfall distribution is the most important factor in differentiating the seasons and climatic regions.
Rainfall occurrence and distribution however, are dependent on the two air masses that prevail over the country.

NIGERIAN CUISINE

Nigerian food is essential to Nigerian culture.
It somewhat defines the Nigerian people.

Although Nigerian cuisine consists of dishes from hundreds of ethnic groups and tribes
in various geographical areas such as the Yoruba, Igbo or Hausa regions,
some dishes are common throughout the entire country including;
Jollof Rice, Fried Rice, Beans Porridge, *Egusi* Soup with Pounded Yam, Coleslaw Salad and *Dodo*.

Like other West African cuisines, Nigerian cooking uses herbs and spices
often in conjunction with palm oil or groundnut oil to create delectable sauces and soups.
Nigerian feasts are colorful and lavish,
while aromatic market and roadside snacks cooked on barbecues are plentiful and varied.

Traditional food is influenced by nations like Portugal, India, Persia, Great Britain and North Africa.
The cuisine of Nigeria is an ancient art that reflects the country's history;
surviving the arrival of the first Europeans (Portuguese) in 1472,
the British invasion of Lagos Island in 1861,
subsequent colonization in 1914,
through to the independence in 1960.

The Nigerian cuisine is infinitely variable and adaptable.
Although fiery and hot, chilli content in most recipes can be reduced or omitted according to taste.
Recipes are passed from mothers to daughters and are rarely written down making each dish a new experience.
Please feel free to adapt recipes according to your taste, to make these recipes part of your permanent collection.

SERVING DINNER IN NIGERIA

Many Nigerians rise as early as 5am to eat a small breakfast and begin their day.
Breakfast usually consists of rice and mangoes, or stewed soybeans.
Dodo (fried plantains) is a common dish, as well as leftovers from the night before.

Lunch is eaten around 11am and is considered the most important meal of the day.
Soups and stews are common lunchtime foods and are often eaten with hands cupped like a spoon.
Many Nigerians only use their right hand.

A late dinner may be served with dishes similar to those offered at lunch.
Most Nigerian meals consist of one course and the dishes are very rich in carbohydrates and protein.
Most meals are cooked outside over an open fire.
Gas and kerosene stoves are sometimes used, but the two fuels are very expensive for many Nigerians.

Dishes such as the following may be served at lunch or dinner.
Coconut rice and *Jollof* rice are Nigeria's well-known rice dishes.
Suya is a meat dish that can be found in almost every part of the country and is often sold as street food.
It is comprised of strips of meat, seasoned with chillies, ground peanuts and local spices, skewered and barbecued.
Egusi soup is a hearty stew made from leafy greens, ground seeds and meat served in many Nigerian households.
Maafe is a well-known dish in Nigeria made with chillies and peanuts.

Fufu is also eaten throughout Nigeria. It is made of yam that has been boiled and pounded until soft.
Meat pies and sausage rolls are fried pastries stuffed with beef or sausage and vegetables.
For dessert Nigerians eat *chin chin* and *puff puff* which are fried, sugared doughnuts.

Palm wine, a natural juice from palm trees, is a favoured drink all over Nigeria,
especially in the south where these trees grow wild.

STAPLE ITEMS

Staple foods in the Nigerian diet include:
peanuts or ground-nuts, yams, cassava, fish, rice, okra, bananas, guinea corn, millet and palm nuts.
Rice, maze and lentil are the staple carbohydrates in Nigerian Food.

Nigerians love to cook with a lot of palm oil, pepper and spices, especially those from the southwest and southeast.

Near the coast of the Gulf of Guinea,
Nigerians prefer eating seafood stews made with fish, shrimp, crab, and lobster, yams, rice, and vegetables.
Fish is important to the Nigerian diet since it is one of only a few sources of protein.

Common meats consumed by the Nigerians are goat, cow, chicken, turkey, mutton, lamb, turkey, geese, pigeon, fish, guinea fowls, crab, shrimp and other seafood.

Common fruits consumed include bananas, oranges, tangerines, pineapples, guavas, watermelons, melons, grapes, limes, mangoes, grapefruits, apples, tomatoes, peas and many more.

The most commonly consumed vegetables are turnip greens, mustard greens, kale, spinach, mushrooms, pumpkins, onions, okra, collard greens, peas, bitter leaf, water leaf, carrots, tomatoes, cabbage and lettuce.

Nigerian herbs and spices are not unique to the African continent, but the variations and uses of the herbs and spices are different from the typical cuisine served in many other areas. Since its climate usually features distinct wet and dry periods, Nigeria can grow spices such as cloves, suya spice, curry spices and bitter leaf. Its cuisine also features coriander, cumin, allspice, ginger, tamarind pods, fennel seeds, mint, thyme, white pepper, cayenne pepper, paprika and nutmeg.

Peppers and chillies are also used regularly in dishes and as a relish.
A Yoruba Proverb says, "The man that eats no pepper is weak, pepper is the staff of life.

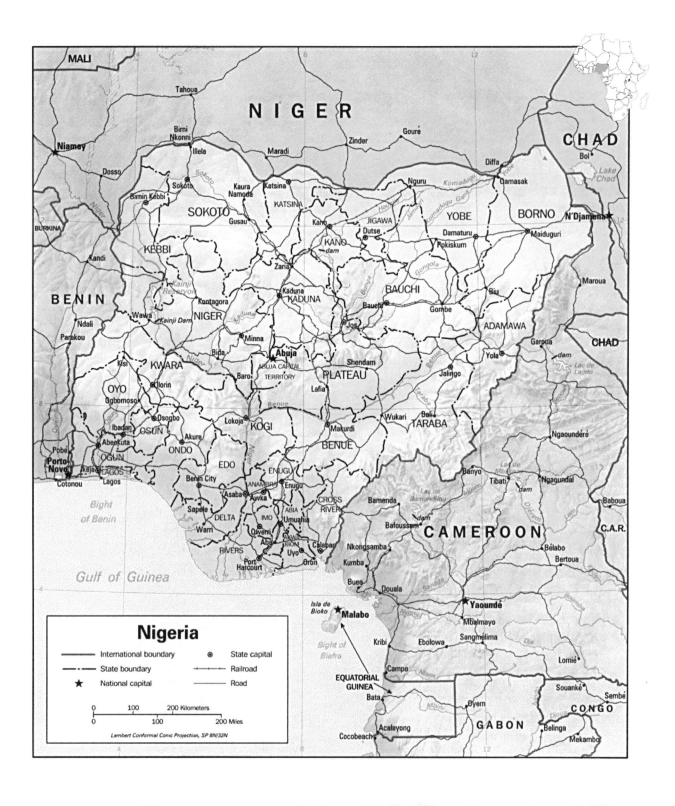

Nigeria

——— International boundary	⊚	State capital
—·—·— State boundary	⊶⊶⊶	Railroad
★ National capital	———	Road

0   100   200 Kilometers
0   100   200 Miles

Lambert Conformal Conic Projection, SP 8N/32N

INDEX

1 - Pepper Soup Seasoning

Description: This is made up of a mixture of local herbs and spices which are not readily available in most supermarkets except in stores specialising in African Foods but similar herbs which can be easily obtained could be used to achieve almost the same effect.

Preparation Time: 5 minutes
Serving Size: 3/4 cup

Substitute Ingredients:

Aniseed	4 tsp
Aniseed pepper	4 tsp
Cloves	2 tsp
Coriander seeds	4 tsp
Cumin seeds	4 tsp
Allspice	4 tsp
Dried ginger	4 tsp
Tamarind pods	4 tsp
Fennel seeds	4 tsp

Traditional Ingredients:

Atariko	4 tsp
Uda	4 tsp
Gbafilo	4 tsp
Ginger (dried)	4 tsp
Rigije	4 tsp
Uyayak	4 tsp

Method:
1.Mix well.

2 - Pepper Soup

Obe Ata

Preparation Time: 10 minutes
Cooking Time: 55 minutes
Serving Size: 6

Ingredients:

Chicken (cut into pieces)	3 lbs
Onions (chopped)	2
Pepper soup seasoning	2 tbsp
Water	1 liter
Tomatoes	3
Red Bell Pepper (optional)	1
Palm Oil	2 tbsp
Salt	to taste
Pepper	to taste

Method:

1. Place the meat, one chopped onion, pepper soup seasoning and water in a pot over medium heat. Boil for 30 minutes.
2. Grind the tomatoes, bell peppers and second onion together. Pour the mixture and palm oil into the pot. Cook over medium-low heat for 25 minutes.
3. Add salt and pepper to taste.

3 - Fish Pepper Soup

Obe Eja Tutu

Preparation Time: 10 minutes
Cooking Time: 30 minutes
Serving Size: 6

Ingredients:

Fish stock	1 liter
Pepper soup seasoning	1 tbsp
Fresh or smoked fish (tilapia, catfish)	2
Lemon juice	1 tsp
Red pepper (cut into fine strips)	1
Green pepper	1/2
Chillies (chopped)	3 tbsp
Tomatoes (skinned, deseeded, diced)	4
Fresh prawns	1 cup
Salt	1/4 tsp
Pepper	1/4 tsp
Mint leaves (chopped)	1/4 cup

Method:

1. Bring the fish stock and pepper soup seasoning to a rapid boil to blend together the flavors.
2. Sprinkle the fish filets with lemon juice and allow to stand for a few minutes. Cut fish into 1 inch cubes.
3. Add red pepper, green pepper, chillies and tomatoes to the boiling fish stock. Cook for 10 minutes, or until tender.
4. Add the fish to the boiling fish stock mixture. Cook for 15 minutes, or until tender. Lower the heat and correct the seasoning with salt and pepper as desired.
5. Serves well garnished with chopped mint leaves.

4 - Pumpkin Seed Soup

Egusi

Description: *Egusi* soup is a hearty stew made from leafy greens, ground seeds and meat that is served for dinner in many Nigerian households. Ground *egusi* seeds give this soup a unique color and flavor. *Egusi* seeds can be purchased from any African store, however if you cannot find, pumpkin seeds will substitute.

Preparation Time: 5 minutes
Cooking Time: 45 minutes
Serving Size: 4

Ingredients:

Ground Egusi	3/4 cup
Tomatoes (chopped)	2
Onion (chopped)	1
Red bell peppers	1
Beef stew meat (cubed)	1 lb
Maggi cubes	2
Salt	1/2 tsp
Palm oil	1/2 cup
Dried crayfish	1/3 cup
Spinach (washed, chopped)	1 lb
Water	as needed

Method:

1. Remove pumpkin seeds from pumpkin a day before and wash and dry. They can also be dried in an oven. When dry, blend until smooth in thick powder form.
2. Blend tomatoes, 1/2 onion and red bell peppers. Set aside.
3. Cook beef with other 1/2 of onion and season with beef seasoning cubes and salt and set aside.
4. Heat palm oil in pot and add blended puree until half cooked. Then add blended egusi to puree and stir fry for 15 minutes.
5. Add beef and crayfish and let cook another 5 minutes.
6. Then add washed chopped spinach and let cook for another 10 minutes. This dish has to have a thick texture, so be mindful of amount of water when cooking.
7. Serves well with fufu.

5 - Okra

Ila

Preparation Time: 3 minutes
Cooking Time: 15 minutes
Serving Size: 4

Ingredients:

Okra	6
Water	

Method:

1.Dice and chop okra into tiny pieces.
2.Place the okra into a pot and add enough water to completely cover it.
3.Cook for 15 minutes.
4.Serves well with obe ata, eba or amala.

6 - Vegetable Soup
Efo

Preparation Time: 5 minutes
Cooking Time: 1 hour, 10 minutes
Serving Size: 6

Ingredients:

Water	
Meat or smoked fish	2 cups
Maggi cubes	2
Palm oil	6 tbsp
Tomatoes	2
Bell pepper	1
Onion	1
Ground crayfish	2 tbsp
Locust beans	1 tbsp
Vegetable leaves (chopped)	1 bunch
Salt	to taste
Pepper	to taste

Method:

1. Boil the meat or fish with salt and maggi cubes until the meat is tender. Set aside.
2. Heat the oil in a pot and fry the meat slightly.
3. Blend the tomatoes, bell peppers and onions.
4. Remove the meat from the oil. Add the blended mixture and crayfish to the oil. Allow to cook for 30 minutes, stirring constantly.
5. Add the meat or smoked fish and simmer for another 20 minutes.
6. Add the locust beans and vegetable leaves and cook for 10 minutes.
7. Add salt and pepper to taste.

7 - Rice Pancakes

Masa

Preparation Time: 10 minutes
Time to Set: 13 hours
Cooking Time: 10 minutes
Serving Size: 12 pancakes

Ingredients:

Basmati Rice	2 cups
Water	
Yeast	1 tsp
Sugar	1 tsp
Baking Powder	a dash
Vegetable oil	

Method:

1. Soak 1 ½ cups of basmati rice in water for 5 hours or more to soften. Then wash and Grind.
2. Wash and boil remaining 1/2 cup of basmati rice until soft. Set aside and allow to cool.
3. Grind/blend soaked rice with boiled rice to a thick paste. Add a teaspoon of yeast to the paste and mix. Cover and allow to rise overnight.
4. With all prep work done, now it's time to fry. Scoop the desired portion size into a bowl, adding sugar if desired or serve sugar on a side plate to accompany your masa. Also add a dash of baking powder to make your masa fluffy.
5. Scoop masa paste into vegetable oil and allow to fry for 2 minutes.
6. Serve masa with suya or eat plain.

8 - Nigerian Salad

Description: Nigerian Salad is unique and exotic. It can be eaten as a meal on its own or as a side dish to *Jollof* Rice, Coconut Rice and other Nigerian dishes. The below ingredients are the minimum for making a Nigerian salad. Additional ingredients such as boiled macaroni, corned beef, green bell pepper and green peas can be added for varied flavour. Heinz Salad Cream works best with the Nigerian Salad, however substitutes are Heinz Caesar Salad Cream or Mayonnaise.

Preparation Time: 15 minutes
Serving Size: 8

Ingredients:

Potatoes	4
Lettuce (cut into thin shreds)	1 bunch
Carrots (peeled, grated)	5
Cucumbers (peeled, cut into strips)	2
Eggs (hard boiled, thinly sliced)	3
Baked beans in tomato sauce	1 ½ cup
Sweet Corn	1 ½ cup
Tomatoes (deseeded, chopped)	5
Salad Dressing (Heinz Salad Cream)	

Method:

1. Place all ingredients into a large bowl in small batches, with the exception of the egg.
2. Place the sliced eggs on the salad, covering the top.
3. Cover the bowl and place in the fridge for at least one hour, allowing ingredients to mix well.
4. Serve with Heinz Salad Cream, Heinz Caesar Salad Cream or Mayonnaise.

9 - Yam Flour

Amala

Cooking Time: 10 minutes
Serving Size: 3

Ingredients:

Elubo (Yam flour)	6 cups
Water	4 cups

Method:

1.Bring the water to a boil.
2.Add the elubo slowly, stirring as you add it.
3.Keep adding it until it is thick. You may not need all of the elubo depending on how thick you want it.
4.Once it is added, continue to mix until it is smooth and consistent in texture.
5.Serve with stew.

10 - Pounded Yam

Iyan

Description: *Iyan* is served as an accompaniment to *egusi* soup, meat or vegetable stews. To eat *iyan*; pull a small ball of mush off with your fingers, form an indentation with your fingers and use to scoop up stews and other dishes, or place large balls in individual serving bowls and spoon stew around them.

Preparation Time: 10 minutes
Cooking Time: 30 minutes
Serving Size: 6

Ingredients:

Raw white yam	2 lbs
Water	

Method:

1. Slice the yams into pieces that are about 1/2 inch in width.
2. Peel the skin off the yams, rinse and place in a pot.
3. Add enough water to cover and cook for 30 minutes, checking every 10 minutes to see if the yams are soft enough for a fork to go through with ease.
4. Drain the yams and put in a morter. Pound with the pestle until it is smooth and forms a soft dough.
5. Place the iyan into a large serving bowl. Wet your hands with water, form into a large ball and serve with stew.

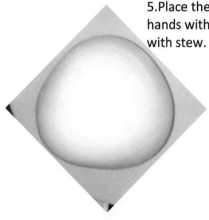

11 - Cassava

Gari

Cooking Time: 10-30 minutes
Serving Size: 2

Ingredients:

Gari	2 cups
Water	as needed
Milk	to taste
Sugar	to taste

Method:

1. Pour gari into a bowl.
2. Add enough water to cover the gari by inch.
3. The impurities of the gari should rise to the top of water. Pour this out.
4. Repeat the rinse process until you are comfortable with it.
5. Serves well with milk or sugar and eaten with a spoon.

12 - Beans Porridge

Preparation Time: 5 minutes
Cooking Time: 1 hour
Serving Size: 6

Ingredients:

African red beans or black eye beans	2 cups
Salt	2 tsp
Tomatoes	2 cups
Red bell peppers	1 cup
Onions	1 cup
Red chilli pepper	1
Red palm oil	4 tbsp
Seasoning cubes (beef or chicken)	2
Chicken or beef broth (optional)	1/2 cup

Method:

1. Cook beans with water and salt until half cooked.
2. Blend tomatoes, peppers, onions and chilli until smooth and set aside.
3. Add blended puree, palm oil, seasoning cubes and chicken or beef broth into half cooked beans.
4. Add water as needed and cook beans with all mixture until you reach desired tenderness.
5. Serves well as a side dish with plain rice, dodo (fried plantains) or stewed chicken.

13 - Meat Pie

Preparation Time: 45 minutes
Cooking Time: 35 minutes
Serving Size: 8 pies

Meat Filling Ingredients:

Vegetable Oil	2 tsp
Onion (diced)	1
Minced meat	1 lb
Cold water	1 ½ cup
Maggi /Knorr cubes	2
Thyme	1 tsp
Carrots (chopped)	2
Potatoes (chopped)	2
Flour	2 tbsp
Salt	to taste

Dough Ingredients:

Plain flour	7 cups
Baking powder	2 tsp
Salt	2 pinches
Margarine (soft)	2 cups
Cold Water	1/2 cup

Meat Filling Method:

1.Heat the vegetable oil in a pot over medium heat, add the onions and stir for 2 minutes.
2.Add the minced meat and stir vigorously until the minced meat turns pale.
3.Add 1 cup of water and the seasoning. Cover the pot and when the contents of the pot start boiling, add the diced carrots and potatoes.
4.When the ingredients are cooked, dissolve flour in half cup of cold water and add to the meat filling.

5.Add salt to taste, stir the contents and remove from heat. Set the meat pie filling aside.

Dough Method:

1.Put the flour in a sizeable bowl. Add baking powder and salt.
2.Spoon the margarine into the bowl of flour.
3.Use your finger tips to rub the margarine into the flour till the mix turns to crumbs.
4.Begin to add cold water in bits while at the same time folding the mix, until a stiff ball is formed.
5.Place the dough on a flat surface, roll it out to a 5mm thickness. If the dough is sticking to the surface, spread dry flour on the surface.
6.Preheat oven to 350°F.
7.Rub margarine on the insides of an oven tray.

Assembly Method:

1.Break the egg, beat it and set aside.
2.Use a cutter to make round cuts on the rolled out dough. Remove the excess dough, leaving behind the round cuts.
3.Scoop some meat pie filling into the center of the round cuts. Rub the egg on the inside edge of the cut dough.
4.Fold one part of the dough to meet the other end and use a fork to press the 2 edges together to close tightly. Place on an oven tray and bake for 35 minutes.

14 - Bean Balls

Akara

Description: These bean fritters appear in several West African countries; they are called *akara* in Nigeria and Sierra Leone and *akla* or *koosé* in Ghana. Although eaten as a snack or side dish, bean fritters are also consumed as breakfast food with hot sauce as an accompaniment.

Preparation Time: 10 minutes
Cooking Time: 10 minutes
Serving Size: 8 fritters

Ingredients:

Dried black-eyed peas	1 cup
Onion (finely chopped)	1/2
Minced habanero chilli (with seeds)	1/4 tsp
Egg	1
Salt	1 tsp
Water	8 tbsp
Palm oil	8 cups

Method:

1. Soak peas in water to cover by 2 inches for 8 hours. Drain in a colander.
2. Purée drained peas, onion, and chilli in a food processor until as smooth as possible. Blend in egg, salt and water until smooth and fluffy. Batter should be just thin enough to drop from a spoon.
3. Heat 2 inches of oil in a 4 inch deep heavy pot. Gently drop batter by tablespoons into hot oil, forming 8 fritters. Fry until golden, about 1 ½ minutes on each side. Transfer to paper towels to drain.

15 - Plantain Chips

Dodo

Preparation Time: 5 minutes
Cooking Time: 15 minutes
Serving Size: 4 cups

Ingredients:

Ripe plantains	4
Salt	to taste
Vegetable oil for deep frying	

Method:

1. Put oil into a frying pan, about 1/2 inch deep. Place over low heat.
2. In a bowl, slice each plantain so that each slice is about 1/4 inch thick.
3. Place the cut pieces into the hot oil, spreading over the bottom of the pan.
4. Turn over when the bottom sides are golden brown in color.
5. Let the other side turn brown to the same consistency as the first side.
6. Remove using a spatula or a large spoon.
7. Drain and place the fried plantains on paper towel to soak up some of the excess oil.
8. Serve as an accompaniment to rice and beans, eggs or a drink.

16 - Beef Kebabs

Suya

Description: *Suya* is a meat dish that can be found in almost every part of the country and is often sold as street food. It is comprised of strips of meat, seasoned with chillies, ground peanuts and local spices, skewered and barbecued.

Preparation Time: 15 minutes
Time to Set: 30 minutes
Cooking Time: 15 minutes
Serving Size: 12 skewers

Ingredients:

Sirloin Steak (cut in strips 5mm x 5cm)	1/2 lb
Ground hot pepper	1 tsp
Salt	1 tsp
Kuli kuli (ground)	1/2 cup
Tomatoes (sliced)	2
Onions (sliced)	2
Skewers for roasting	

Method:

1. Mix the ground hot pepper, salt and kuli kuli together.
2. Put the meat inside the mixture and ensure each piece is well covered.
3. When ready to cook, thread the beef strips onto soaked wooden skewers, with the meat stretched out and not bunched up. Add the sliced tomatoes and sliced onions between the pieces of meat.
4. Cook on a grill pan or the Barbeque.
5. Let cook for a few minutes and then turn to cook the other side. The meat should be cooked in 10 minutes, depending on the thickness of your meat slices.
6. Remove from heat and allow to rest for an hour.

17 - Spicy Skewered Meat Kebabs

Tsiren Dakakken Nama

Preparation Time: 15 minutes
Time to Set: 1 hour
Cooking Time: 10 minutes
Serving Size: 4

Ingredients:

Lean mince beef	1 lb
Chilli powder	1 tsp
Onion (finely chopped)	1
Egg (beaten)	1
Coriander (chopped)	2 tbsp
Nutmeg	1 tsp
Salt	to taste
Oil for brushing	

Method:

1.Put all the ingredients except the oil in a large bowl and mix together with fork. Cover and refrigerate the mixture for 1 hour.

2.Light the Barbecue or grill pan. Divide the mixture into 12 equal portions. Shape each portion into a sausage about 2 inches long, squeezing each sausage firmly to make it compact.

3.Push the kebab skewers and through the sausage, moulding them firmly on the skewer. Brush kebab with oil and place on the grill.

4.Cook kebab for 10 minutes, turning frequently.

5.Serves well garnished with lemon slices, with salads or on jollof rice with hot sauce.

18 - Coconut Rice

Preparation Time: 15 minutes
Cooking Time: 20-50 minutes
Serving Size: 6

Ingredients:

Coconuts	2
Onion (sliced)	1
Black pepper	to taste
Rice	3 cups
Maggi cube	1
Salt	to taste
Water	

Method:

1. Break your coconut and remove the shell.
2. Cut coconut into sizable piece, pour into blender, add water and blend till smooth.
3. To get the juice, sieve and throw away the chaff. Pour the coconut juice in a pot.
4. Add onion and pepper. Bring to boil.
5. Add your rice and maggi cube. Salt to taste.
6. Reduce heat and cook until rice is soft, adding water if needed.

For Variation:

1. Sliced tomatoes can also be added.

19 - Jollof Rice

Description: *Jollof* is rice cooked with ground tomatoes, peppers and sometimes meat and vegetables. *Jollof* rice probably originated from rice dishes eaten by the Wolof people of Senegal and Gambia, but its popularity has spread to most of West Africa, especially Nigeria and Ghana.

Preparation Time: 10 minutes
Cooking Time: 50 minutes
Serving Size: 6

Ingredients:

White rice	4 cups
Water	6 cups
Tomatoes (chopped)	2
Red bell peppers (chopped)	1
Onions (chopped)	1
Cayenne pepper	1 tbsp
Salt	a pinch

Method:

1.Rince rice. Place the rice and water into a pot over medium-high heat and cook.

2.Blend the tomatoes, pepper and onion until they are smooth in texture. Mix in cayenne pepper.

3.Add the tomato/pepper/onion mixture to the rice after rice has been cooking for 15 minutes.

4.Add enough water to allow the rice to complete cooking.

5.Drain cooked rice.

6.Serves well with stewed chicken, beef or fish.

20 - Fried Rice

Description: Rice is widely eaten in Nigeria and there are many different types to chose from. It is prepared, cooked and served in an attractive variety. However, boiled white rice is plain when eaten on its own, so it is always served as accompaniments to soups and stews or as an all in one dish with fish, meat and vegetables mixed. Nigerians love this dish with assorted beef or chicken stew and coleslaw salad.

Preparation Time: 15 minutes
Cooking Time: 50 minutes
Serving Size: 8

Ingredients:

Long grain rice	3 cups
Chicken or beef broth	4 cups
Carrots	2
Red bell peppers	1/2 cup
Green bell peppers	1/2 cup
Onions	2
Canola oil	3 tbsp
Sweet corn	2/3 cup
Peas	2/3 cup
Seasoning cubes (chicken or beef)	2
Curry	1 tbsp
Salt	a pinch

Method:

1. Cook long grain rice with water and chicken broth until tender and set aside.
2. Cut carrots, red and green bell peppers and onions into small bite size cubes and set aside.
3. Add canola oil into a stir fry pan.
4. Stir fry carrots, green and red bell peppers, onions, sweet corn and peas. Add seasoning cubes of any flavor, curry and salt.
5. When cooked to desired texture, add mixture into long grain rice and mix well.

21 - Palm Oil Stew

Alapa

Description: This is the real traditional stew commonly served in the villages and by the roadside food hawkers. The use of palm-oil makes this stew particularly mouth watering.

Preparation Time: 5 minutes
Cooking Time: 30 minutes
Serving Size: 6

Ingredients:

Beef (cubed)	2 lbs
Salt	to taste
Medium size onions (chopped)	2
Water	4 cups
Palm-oil	1/2 cup
Tomatoes (chopped)	5 cups
Fresh peppers (chopped)	1 cup
Tomato puree	1 ½ cups

Method:

1. Place the cubed pieces of meat in a pot with salt, onions and water. Cook over medium-high heat for 10 minutes.
2. Heat the palm oil in a pot over medium heat and fry the tomatoes and peppers for 5 minutes.
3. Add the tomato puree to the palm oil mixture and stir thoroughly.
4. Drain the cooked meat and onions and add to the palm oil mixture. Stir thoroughly and simmer for 15 minutes.
5. Remove from heat and serve with boiled rice or yam.

22 - Spinach and Peanut Stew
Maafe

Description: *Maafe* is a traditional sub-Saharan African recipe for a classic sauce of spinach with ground peanuts and flavoured with hot chillies. This sticky stew is intended to be eaten with *FuFu* or rice.

Preparation Time: 5 minutes
Cooking Time: 40 minutes
Serving Size: 6

Ingredients:

Oil for frying	2 tbsp
Scotch bonnet chillies (pounded)	2 tbsp
Spinach	15 cups
Peanuts (coarsely ground)	1 ½ cups
Oil	2 tbsp
Salt	1/2 tsp
Black pepper	1/4 tsp

Method:

1. In a heavy-bottomed pan, add the oil and heat until almost smoking.
2. Fry the chillies for 3 minutes then add the spinach. Stirring constantly, wilt the spinach then add just enough water to cover.
3. After 4 minutes sprinkle in the peanuts and stir-in well. Cover and continue to cook over medium heat for about 30 minutes, adding more water if necessary to prevent burning.
4. Drain and mix in the oil, salt and pepper.

23 - Chicken Stew

Preparation Time: 10 minutes
Cooking Time: 55 minutes
Serving Size: 6

Ingredients:

Whole chicken (cut into chunks)	1
Curry	1 tsp
Thyme	1 tsp
Salt	to taste
Ginger	1 tbsp
Garlic cloves	2
Onions (sliced)	4
Tomatoes	5 cups
Red bell pepper	1
Red chilli	1
Canola oil	2 cups
Seasoning cubes (chicken or beef)	2

Method:

1. Steam chicken with curry, thyme, salt, ginger, garlic and half of the sliced onions. Cook until chicken is tender but not too soft.
2. Remove the chicken from broth and grill in oven until golden brown.
3. Blend Tomatoes, red bell pepper, red chilli and onions and set aside.
4. Put oil in a pot and when hot, pour in blended puree. Stir fry for 30 minutes.
5. Add the grilled chicken and chicken broth to the oil. Cook puree with chicken and chicken broth for 10 minutes.
6. Serves well with plain rice, jollof rice or fried rice and fried plantains.

For Variation:

1. Garnish with sliced onions, red and green bell peppers.
2. Add chopped spinach into the puree for a healthier choice.
3. Beef or fish can be used as well.

24 - Beef and Spinach Stew

Shoko

Description: This is a classic Yoruban recipe from Nigeria. *Shoko* is a green leaf used commonly in Yoruban cooking. It wilts easily and is typically replaced by spinach, though a mix of spinach and dandelion leaves would be closer to the original. *Egusi* seeds are a variant form of watermelon seeds and are extensively cultivated in Nigeria for the high protein and carbohydrate content of the edible seeds. They are often added as a thickener to stews.

Preparation Time: 5 minutes
Cooking Time: 1 hour, 25 minutes
Serving Size: 6

Ingredients:

Beef (cubed)	1 lb
Olive oil	3 tbsp
Onions (chopped)	2
Scotch bonnet chilli (chopped)	1
Tomatoes (chopped)	8
Egusi seeds (ground)	1/2 cup
Water	1 cup
Spinach (washed, torn)	8 cups
Salt	1 tsp
Ginger (grated)	1/2 tsp

Method:

1. In a large pan, fry the beef in the oil until well browned.
2. Add the onions, chilli and tomatoes and simmer for 5 minutes, until the tomatoes begin to break down.
3. Add the egusi seeds and water. Then reduce to a low simmer and cook for 1 hour.
4. Add the spinach, salt and ginger. Simmer for 10 minutes before serving on a bed of rice.

25 - Spinach and Egg Stew

Preparation Time: 5 minutes
Cooking Time: 25 minutes
Serving Size: 6

Ingredients:

Onion	1
Tomatoes	8
Chilli pepper	4
Garlic clove	1
Groundnut oil	6 tbsp
Tomato puree	4 tbsp
Thyme	1 tsp
Iru locust bean	1 tsp
Salt	to taste
Spinach (blanched, chopped)	2 lbs
Soft boiled egg	8

Method:

1. Grind the onions, tomatoes, chillies and garlic.
2. Heat the oil in a pot, then add the grinded ingredients and cook for 15 minutes.
3. Add tomato puree, thyme, iru and salt while stirring thoroughly. The sauce should be fairly thick.
4. Add the chopped spinach and soft boiled eggs. Stir and simmer for 5 minutes.
5. Serve hot with boiled rice.

26 - Bread

Agege

Description: Bread is eaten with every meal in Nigerian cuisine. The best bread to eat, is often the subject of a good-natured argument. Oyo bread is favored by some, while thousands of loaves of this sweet, heavy *agege* bread are sold each day throughout Nigeria, especially in the capital city of Lagos.

Preparation Time: 40 minutes
Time to Set: 5 hours
Cooking Time: 35 minutes
Serving Size: 2 loaves

Ingredients:

Dry yeast (one small packet)	1 tbsp
Water	1/4 cup
Milk	2 cups
Sugar	2 tbsp
Salt	2 tsp
Shortening	1 tbsp
Bread flour (sifted)	6 cups

Method:

1. Sprinkle dry yeast in warm water.
2. Scald milk in a sauce pan, then remove from heat. Add sugar, salt and shortening to the milk. Cool to lukewarm.
3. Add yeast/water mixture to the milk mixture and 2 cups of sifted flour. Beat with a hand mixer on lowest speed.
4. Stir in 2 to 3 more cups of flour.
5. When dough becomes too stiff to stir, turn out on to well floured surface. Knead for 10 minutes, or until smooth. Add flour to the kneading surface as needed to prevent the dough from becoming sticky. Shape into a ball.
6. Put into a large greased bowl, turning over to coat the entire surface. Cover with warm damp towel, then place another towel over that and place in a warm place. Let rise until doubled, about 1 ½ hours.
7. Punch down. Let rise again until doubled, about 45 minutes.
8. Divide dough into 2 pieces and shape each into a ball placing on floured surface. Cover and let bread rest for 10 minutes.
9. Grease 2 loaf pans.
10. Flatten balls into long rectangles about 8x16 inches. Roll up lengthwise shaping into loaves to fit pan. Cover and let rise for 1 hour, until doubled in size.
11. Bake at 400°F for 35 minutes, covering with foil for the last 20 minutes, if the tops get too brown.
12. When bread is done, remove from pans at once, placing on a wire rack to cool.

27 - Round Donuts
Puff Puff

Preparation Time: 5 minutes
Cooking Time: 20 minutes
Serving Size: 40-60 balls

Ingredients:

Flour	2 cups
Sugar	1/2 cup
Water	2 cups
Yeast	2 tsp
Vegetable oil for deep frying	

Method:

1.Mix the flour, sugar, water and yeast together until the batter is smooth.
2.Let the dough rise for 2 ½ hours.
3.Place vegetable oil into a pot, until it is at least 2 inches high. Place over low heat.
4.Test oil to make sure it is hot enough by putting a drop of batter into the oil. If it is not hot enough, the batter will stay at the bottom of the pot rather than rising to the top.
5.When the oil is hot enough, use one spoon to scoop the batter and another spoon to drop it into the oil, in the shape of a ball.
6.Fry for a few minutes until the bottom side is golden brown.
7.Turn the ball over and fry for a few more minutes until the other side is golden brown.
8.Use a large spoon to remove donuts from the oil. Place on paper towel to soak up some of the excess oil.
9.If desired, roll the balls in sugar or powdered sugar to make them sweeter.
10.Serves well hot or cold.

28 - Hibiscus Punch

Zobo

Description: *Zobo* is a tart tasting herbal infusion/tea with a very unique taste.

Preparation Time: 3 minutes
Time to Set: 1 hour
Cooking Time: 5 minutes
Serving Size: 15 cups

Ingredients:

Dried hibiscus flowers	2 cups
Water	9 cups
Pineapple juice	4 cups
Vanilla extract	2 tbsp
Honey	1 cup
Sugar	1/4 cup
Extra water	2 cups

Method:

1. Lightly rinse the hibiscus flowers in cold water.

2. Pour 9 cups of water into a pot and bring to a boil. As soon as it starts boiling, remove from the stove.

3. Put the rinsed flowers into the hot water. Cover and let steep for 1 hour.

4. Put a paper towel on the inside of a sieve. Get a large deep bowl ready and drain mixture. Be sure that the flower sediments don't go into the bowl.

5. Pour the drained mixture into a pitcher. Add pineapple juice and vanilla extract.

6. Taste for sweetness, adding honey and sugar.

7. Stir and refrigerate.

I am only one, but I am one. I cannot do everything, but I can do something. And I will not let what I cannot do interfere with what I can do. -Edward Everett Hale

Of the 40 million inhabitants in Kenya, 42 percent are under the age of 15.
Per capita income in Kenya averages $360 USD per year.
38 percent of Kenya's rural population does not have access to clean drinking water.
75 percent of Kenyans are farmers, but have low agricultural productivity.

Kenya is also a country with many stories of talents, skills, ideas, imagination, drive and excellence.
In this section we share some of that excellence as it pertains to
the unique traditions and outstanding flavours of Kenyan Cuisine.
Join us as we celebrate the country of Kenya!

We can do no great things, only small things with great love. -Mother Theresa

THE COUNTRY OF KENYA

Kenya is an East African country that is home to 40 million people.
It is located on the equator, with Somalia to the northeast, the Indian Ocean to the southeast, Tanzania to the south,
Uganda to the west, South Sudan to the northwest and Ethiopian to the north.
It spans 224,080 square miles (580,367 square kilometers), making it a little smaller than the province of Quebec.
Kenya's capital and largest city is Nairobi with a population of 3.5 million.

Kenya is bursting with intrigue;
from the fascinating rituals and jewelry of the Maasai tribe,
to the magnificent animals such as lions, giraffes, leopards, antelopes, zebras, elephants and rhinoceros
living on the Savanna grasslands between the tropical rainforests and the majestic desert.

Although the most well known tribe in Kenya is the Maasai, there are more than 40 different tribes.
The oldest human-like fossils ever found, were discovered in Kenya.

Kenya was called the British East African Protectorate until 1920. It was then named after Mount Kenya.
Kenya gained independence from Britain on December 12, 1963.
The country has significant ethnic diversity and the official languages are Swahili and English.

Kenya's landscape ranks among the most enthralling and varied in the world.
From the low-lying coastlands,
to Mount Kenya towering at 17,058 ft above sea level,
as the second highest mountain of the African continent after Kilimanjaro.
From the open, grassy plains,
to the sudden drop into the floor of the eastern arm of the Great Rift Valley with its lakes nestled in the valley floor,
in a landscape decorated by dramatic escarpments, volcanic cones and hot springs.

With such contrasting scenery, Kenya also has a varied climate.
The hot and humid coastal belt contrasts to the highlands, where temperatures could be as low as 5 degrees celcius.
The Lake Victoria region sees tropical storms while the north has a desert climate,
where rain at times does not fall for up to one year.

KENYAN CUISINE

Though the food of this great African nation is outstanding, it is not well known.
From Mombasa on the east coast to Lake Victoria in the west,
Kenya has a varied and nutritious cuisine awaiting your discovery.

Perhaps the most delightful feature of Kenyan food is its diverse flavor.
Kenyan cooking draws from a variety of ethnic traditions,
and combines them with the seasonings of outside countries.
Due to Kenya's colonization by the British and history with foreign settlers,
the taste, cooking methods and presentation of Kenyan foods have been influenced significantly
by Indians, Arabs, Europeans, and Pakistanis as well as some western countries.

Recipes are also often reflective of the different regions of Kenya.
Foods from the coastal areas of the Indian Ocean and Lake Victoria reflect the Arabic influence
where rice and fish, flavored with coconut, tamarind and exotic spices are relished.
Foods from the rural country contain more beef, chicken, goat, fish, rice and vegetables.

Corn is a staple in Kenya and appears in many forms and dishes.

Vegetables are a large part of the Kenyan diet and are served as main dishes, sides and condiments.

The warm climate of Kenya provides for a long and fruitful growing season along the coast
and in the southern region where there is an abundance of tropical fruits.
Coconuts are plentiful in the coastal regions,
and oranges, lemons, mangos, pears, papaws, bananas and pineapples are common.

Additional local yields include;
tea, coffee, ginger, rice wheat, sweet potatoes, highland vegetables, sugar cane, bananas, pineapples and tropical
fruits, fresh beef and lamb, every kind of seafood, wine, beer, maize, millet and sunflowers.

SERVING DINNER IN KENYA

Two menus represent the foods of a typical Kenyan *chakula* (meal).
Irio is the mainstay in one and in the other it is *Ugali*.
In the homes of the Kikuyu, the mainstay is *Irio*,
followed by dishes like *Giteke* (bananas and yams), *Karanga* (beef and potato stew) and *Mataha* (beans and corn).
In the homes of the Abaluhya, the important course is *Ugali*,
followed by dishes like *M'baazi* (pea beans), *M'chuzi Wa Kuku* (coconut chicken) or *Samaki Na Nazi* (coconut fish).

At *chakula cha asubuhi* (breakfast), a semisweet, flat doughnut called *Maandazi* is frequently eaten,
with *kahawa* or *chai* (coffee and tea in Swahili).
Kenyans also eat *chapattis* at breakfast and usually dip it in their coffee.

Lunch is the main *chakula* of the day.
Meats such as beef, goat or mutton (sheep) are most regularly consumed.

Foods served at dinner are similar to foods served at lunch.
If attending a Kenyan home for a traditional meal, your experience would likely be as follows.
The hostess would open the door with her arms outstretched to greet you.
She is dressed in a long, bright skirt with a striking bandanna wound loosely on her head.
Before the meal, the hostess goes to each person with a pitcher of water, a plastic bowl, soap and a towel
so that everyone can wash their hands before they eat.
To begin the meal, she first brings in a pot of tea which she serves in small cups with tiny bananas.
She then serves soup and afterward, all of the remaining dishes are placed on the table at the same time,
each in a beautifully decorated bowl called a *calabash*.
After the meal, the hostess will usually bring around the bowl so that everyone can wash their hands again.
Dessert is generally not served, and includes fresh fruit.
The after-dinner beverage is *Chai* or sour skimmed milk.

Mealtime customs can vary from region to region and tribe to tribe.
Some warriors will not eat in front of women, men are served first and children often eat separately from adults.

STAPLE ITEMS

The most admired foods in Kenya are fresh foods from the country's vast resources.
Farmland, lakes and the Indian Ocean provide readily available vegetables, fruits and meats.

Commonly consumed vegetables are kale, spinach, cabbage, tomatoes, beans, potatoes and avocados.

Commonly consumed fruits include mangoes, oranges, pineapples, bananas, papaws and pears,
with availability varying by season.

Commonly served meats in a Kenyan meal are beef and goat.
Fish, chicken and mutton are also available but more expensive.
Adventurous meat eaters can also indulge in safe wildlife game meat,
such as crocodile and ostrich served in specialized restaurants,
however game meat is rarely eaten in Kenyan homes.

Other ingredients used in typical Kenyan dishes and recipes include rice, corn meal, wheat and millet flour.

Essential spices in Kenyan cooking are;
cardamom, cumin, whole peppercorns, whole cloves, dried chillies,
salt, pepper, turmeric, cayenne pepper, tamarind, nutmeg, cinnamon,
gingerroot, basil, thyme, oregano, parsley and coriander.

Kenyans are avid tea drinkers, thus hot beverages such as Kenyan tea and coffee are often served with meals.
Cold beverages like soda, juice and domestic and international beers are also available
in restaurants, hotels, pubs and entertainment spots,
in addition to Tusker, which is the beer of choice for most Kenyans.

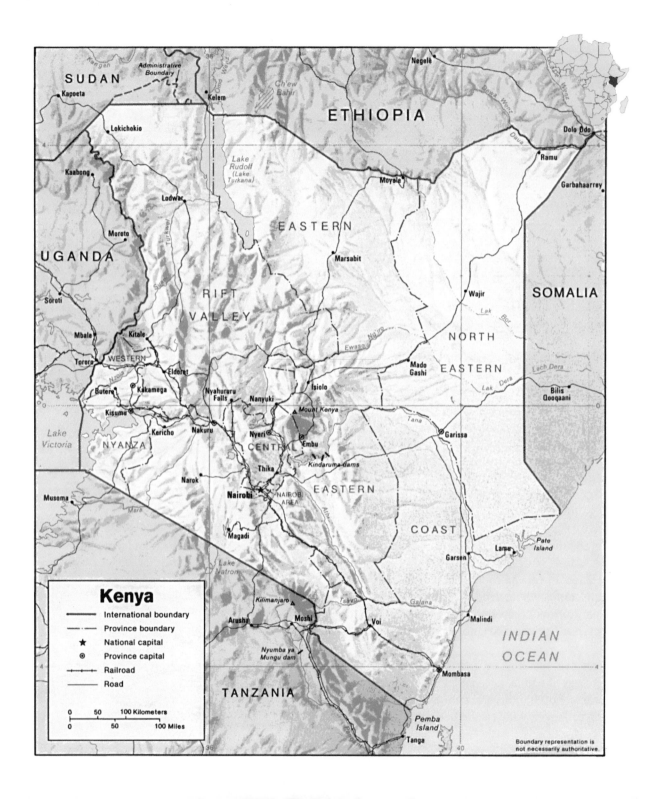

INDEX

1 - Fried Vegetable Turnover

Mboga Sambusa

Description: Street vendors can be found on most street corners in Kenya offering a variety of snacks. *Sambusas* are deep-fried pastry triangles stuffed with spiced minced vegetables and meats.

Preparation Time: 45 minutes
Cooking Time: 15 minutes
Serving Size: 20 sambusas

Filling Ingredients:

Vegetable oil	1 tbsp
Mustard seeds	1/4 tsp
Sesame seeds	1/4 tsp
Medium onion (finely chopped)	1
Fresh coriander (chopped)	1 tbsp
Lemon juice	1 tbsp
Cumin	1 tsp
Salt	1/2 tsp
Chilli powder	a pinch
Potatoes (boiled, peeled, chopped)	3
Peas	1/4 cup

Filling Method:

1. Heat the vegetable oil, mustard seeds and sesame seeds in a skillet.
2. When the seeds pop, add the onion and coriander. Sauté until the onion becomes translucent.
3. Add lemon juice, cumin, salt and chilli powder. Sauté for 3 minutes.
4. Add potatoes and peas. Mix well and sauté just until heated through, then remove from heat and set aside.

Dough Ingredients:

White flour	2 cups
Vegetable oil	2 ½ tbsp
Rice flour	1 ½ tbsp
Salt	1/2 tsp

Dough Method:

1. Mix flour, vegetable oil, rice flour and salt.
2. Add water gradually (about 1/4 cup) until the dough hold together and knead well.
3. Roll into a ball and cover with a moist cloth. Let rest for 20 minutes.

Assembly Method:

1. To assemble the sambusas, break off 2 inch pieces of dough and roll into 6 inch circles.
2. Cut each circle in half. Fold each half circle in thirds to make a pie wedge shape. Seal the point by pressing and pinching. Pick up the dough and seal the outside edge by pinching to form a cone.
3. Fill the cone 2/3 with potato mixture. Moisten the lip of the cone with a little water, and pinch to seal.
4. Heat the oil in a pan and deep-fat fry sambusas a few at the time until they are golden brown.

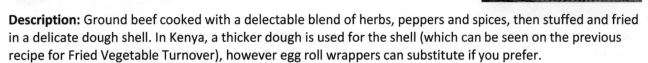

2 - Fried Meat Turnover

Nyama Sambusa

Description: Ground beef cooked with a delectable blend of herbs, peppers and spices, then stuffed and fried in a delicate dough shell. In Kenya, a thicker dough is used for the shell (which can be seen on the previous recipe for Fried Vegetable Turnover), however egg roll wrappers can substitute if you prefer.

Preparation Time: 20 minutes
Cooking Time: 40 minutes
Serving Size: 50 sambusas

Ingredients:

Garlic cloves	6
1 Inch ginger root	1
Large onions	3
Ground lamb or beef	2 lbs
Curry powder	1 tbsp
Turmeric	1 tbsp
Garam masala	1 tbsp
Salt	to taste
Egg-roll dough	2 lbs
Flour	
Oil	

Method:

1. Put the garlic and ginger in a blender and blend them until they're well mashed.
2. Thinly slice the onions and combine them with the ginger, garlic, meat, curry powder, turmeric and garam masala. Mix well.
3. Take a heavy frying pan and sauté without adding any fat over a low heat for 30 minutes. Stir occasionally to break up the meat.
4. Salt to taste.
5. Cut the thawed egg-roll dough into strips of 3 by 6 inches. Make a triangular pocket of each strip by folding one point up. Fold over again and fill the pocket with a bit of the meat mixture you just made. Bring down the top, then seal all the open sides with a paste made of water and flour. You should now have a meat-stuffed pastry in triangle shape.
6. Heat the oil in a pan and deep-fat fry the sambusas a few at the time until they are golden brown.
7. Drain the sambusas before serving.
8. Serve with chutney.

3 - Pea Soup
M'baazi Supu

Preparation Time: 15 minutes
Cooking Time: 25 minutes
Serving Size: 4

Ingredients:

Onion (finely chopped)	1
Celery (finely chopped)	1/2 cup
Olive oil	1 tbsp
Potato (cooked, chopped)	1
Ham (cubed)	1 ¼ cup
Lemon peel (grated)	a pinch
Chicken stock	1 ½ cups
Peas (drained)	2 cups
Fresh basil	1/4 cup
Fresh parsley	1/4 cup
Natural applesauce	1/2 cup
Sour cream	1/2 cup
Butter	2 tbsp
Coriander	1/2 tsp
Nutmeg	1/4 tsp
Tabasco	5 drops
Worcestershire sauce	3 squirts
Black pepper	to taste
Parmesan cheese	for garnish

Method:

1. In a saucepan, fry the onion and celery in olive oil.
2. Add the potato, ham, lemon peel, chicken stock and peas. Simmer for 3 minutes.
3. Add the basil, parsley, applesauce, sour cream and butter. Simmer for 5 minutes.
4. Add the coriander, nutmeg, tabasco, worcestershire sauce and pepper. Adjust to your taste.
5. Let the broth cool.
6. Purée half of the soup in a processor, leaving the other half of the broth as it is.
7. Return the thick puree to the broth and stir.
8. Reheat the soup.
9. To serve, pour into bowls and garnish with parmesan cheese.

4 - African Coleslaw

Kachumbari

Description: *Kachumbari* is a cold side dish of chopped vegetables in a vinegar or lemon juice dressing. This is a lovely side dish known to some as African coleslaw.

Preparation Time: 10 minutes
Serving Size: 1 bowl

Ingredients:

Tomatoes (thinly sliced)	5
Small onions (thinly sliced)	2
Red chilli (de-seeded, cut into slivers)	1
Coriander (finely chopped)	1/2 cup
Lime (juiced)	1
Olive oil	3 tbsp
Salt	to taste
Black pepper	to taste

Method:

1.Place the sliced tomatoes, onions, chilli and chopped coriander into a large serving bowl.
2.Add the lime juice and olive oil and toss evenly into the mixture.
3.Season with the salt and freshly ground black pepper.
4.Serves well with mchele pilau.

5 - Coconut Rice

Wali

Description: *Wali* is rice boiled in coconut milk. Along the Kenyan coast, *wali* is a popular meal of the Swahili and Mijikenda tribes. Palm trees grow across Kenya's coastline and fresh coconut is always readily available.

Preparation Time: 5 minutes
Cooking Time: 35 minutes
Serving Size: 6

Ingredients:

Rice	2 cups
Salt	a pinch
Thin coconut milk	4 cups
Thick coconut milk	2 tbsp

Method:

1. Put the rice, salt and thin coconut milk in a pot.
2. Bring to a boil, reduce heat, and simmer very gently for 30 minutes, until the rice is done.
3. Watch the pot, adding more thin coconut milk if the rice becomes dry.
4. Just before serving, add the thick coconut milk and stir.
5. Serves well with beef or chicken stew and vegetables of your choice.

6 - Rice Pilaf

Mchele Pilau

Description: A fantastic rice dish that is traditional to Kenya. This recipe is a beautiful example of the fusion between African and Indian cuisines local to the area.

Preparation Time: 5 minutes
Cooking Time: 1 hour
Serving Size: 6

Ingredients:

Goat or beef (cubed)	1 lb
Garlic cloves	4
Cardamom pods	9
Large onion (chopped)	1
Vegetable oil	4 tbsp
Rice	3 cups
Whole black peppercorns	10
Whole cloves	8
Cinnamon sticks	8
Ground ginger	1 tsp
Cumin	1/4 cup
Small tomatoes	4
Water	6 cups
Salt	to taste

Method:

1. Boil the meat in salted water until tender.
2. Crush the garlic and cardamom together with 2 tbsp of water.
3. Sauté the onion in oil until it is golden brown.
4. Add the rice, meat, peppercorns, cloves, cinnamon, ginger and cumin to the garlic and cardamom mixture. Cook covered over medium heat for 10 minutes, until all are nicely brown.
5. Add the tomatoes. Cook and stir until the tomatoes are thoroughly cooked down to the consistency of a sauce.
6. Add the 6 cups water to the rice mixture, bring to a boil and then cover and cook over very low heat, for 20 minutes, until all water is absorbed and the rice is cooked through.
7. Serves well with kachumbari.

7 - White Cornmeal

Ugali

Description: *Ugali* is known as the national dish and eaten by most tribes of Kenya. Authentic Kenyan *Ugali* is strictly a mix of white corn flour and boiling water only, with no additional ingredients required. Kenyan *Ugali* is white in color and served as a traditional Kenyan accompaniment to meat and vegetable stews which are poured over it.

Cooking Time: 15 minutes
Serving Size: 6

Ingredients:

Boiling water	4 cups
White corn flour	2 cups
Salt	optional

Method:

1. Bring water to a boil.
2. Reduce heat to medium and add flour gradually, stirring continuously until the consistency is stiff. Cover for about 5 minutes.
3. Stir again and form into a mound. The ugali is done when it pulls from the sides of the pan easily and does not stick.
4. Serves well with Sukuma Wiki, fish or meat.

8 - Corn and Peas Mash

Irio

Description: Both the Kikuyu and Meru people lay claim to this recipe. *Irio* is a hearty and nutritious accompaniment to meals, that has become popular throughout Kenya. It has many variations, but potatoes and peas are the staple ingredients with corn the most common addition. *Irio* is famously paired with grilled steak in the combination known as *nyama na irio*. As butter is a luxury product in Kenya, families more commonly use corn oil or peanut butter oil.

Preparation Time: 5 minutes
Cooking Time: 20 minutes
Serving Size: 6

Ingredients:		Method:
Corn cobs	4	1.Remove the corn kernels from the cobs and boil with peas in a pot until soft.
Green peas	2 cups	
Medium potatoes (peeled)	4	2.Add potatoes and pumpkin leaves. Boil together until the potatoes are cooked. Drain, add salt and mash.
Pumpkin leaves or spinach	2 bunches	
Salt	to taste	
Medium onion (chopped)	1	3.Sauté the onion in butter.
Butter	1 tbsp	4.Add curry powder and mix into the mash. Stir well until it is a smooth, soft mixture.
Curry powder	1 tsp	

9 - Tea
Chai

Description: Tea was first introduced in Kenya in 1903. Commercialization of tea started in 1924 and since then, Kenya can boast itself as major producer of black tea. Kenya is one of the world's top producers and exporters of tea, ranked 3rd behind China and India.

Kenya's fertile soils and sunny but cool uplands make it the perfect environment for the cultivation of high quality teas. The tea is grown in the rich highlands of Kenya and over 186,000 hectares are used, producing over 260,000,000 kg of tea a year. 90 percent of this production is exported in bulk.

Kenyan Teas are famous for their brightness, attractive colour, brisk flavour and textures of fragrant leaves. Traditionally used in blending, African teas are now emerging in their own right in the specialty market. Although most tea produced in Kenya is Black tea, green, yellow and white teas are also produced.

Chai is Swahili for tea. Kenyan culture is embracing of many different cultures, with tea time being borrowed from the British and the style of tea being borrowed from India. *Chai* is tea with milk and sugar in Kenya. Other names for *chai* in Kenya are; spiced tea, spiced milk tea, milk tea or tea latte. *Chai* is served at breakfast, morning break, after lunch, afternoon tea and after dinner, as the beverage choice of Kenya.

Cooking Time: 15 minutes
Serving Size: 1 cup

Ingredients:		Method:
Water	1 cup	1.Combine water and tea leaves together in a saucepan. Boil for 10 minutes on high heat.
Tea leaves	1 ½ tsp	
Milk	1 cup	2.Add milk and heat to near boiling.
Sugar	2 to 4 tsp	3.Add sugar to taste.

10 - Unleavened Flatbread

Chapati

Description: *Chapati* is a round, flat unleavened bread cooked on a skillet to a soft brown color. It is often served with meat stew and vegetables. *Chapati* was introduced to Kenyan cuisine by the large Indian community living in Kenya for decades and has proven to be very popular.

Preparation Time: 1 hour, 25 minutes
Cooking Time: 10 minutes
Serving Size: 12 chapatis

Ingredients:

Whole wheat flour	1 cup
White flour	1 cup
Salt	1 tsp
Oil	2 tbsp
Warm water	3/4 cup

Method:

1. Mix the whole wheat flour and white flour together in a bowl.
2. Add salt and oil. Mix with hands or use a mixer.
3. Add a little bit of water at a time and knead well for 10 minutes until you have a stiff and smooth dough.
4. Cover the dough and let it stand for 1 hour.
5. Knead the dough well again and divide it into egg-sized balls. Dust each ball with extra flour. Flatten each ball and roll out thinly into sizeable circles.
6. Heat an ungreased, heavy skillet over a medium flame.
7. Lightly grease the pan and slowly heat the first chapati.
8. Cook on one side for about 1 minute or until lightly brown, then flip and brown the other side. Press the sides of the chapati with a spoon until it puffs up.
9. Remove the chapati from the skillet into a warm dish or foil paper and wrap to keep chapatis warm.
10. Repeat this process for every chapati, wiping the pan with greased paper every time a new chapati is to be cooked.
11. Serves well warm with a meat stew or cooked vegetables. Chapatis can also be served with hot milk or chai.

11 - Corn and Beans
Githeri

Description: Apart from *ugali*, *githeri* is one of the main staple foods in Kenya. *Githeri* is a simple yet nourishing dish that originated with Kikuyu tribe. In modern times it has become popular throughout Kenya. There are several variations of this mixture that may include adding peas, groundnuts, potatoes and vegetables.

Turmeric is originally an Indian spice and need only be added if you want additional flavor or if you want it to be more exotic. Also note that the beans are usually Kenyan kidney beans and the corn used (usually called *maindi*) takes quite a while to soften, as they are hard. If you don't have Kenyan kidney beans or *maindi*, you can buy the equivalent in an African grocery store or at the grocery, but the cooking time will vary. *Githeri* is usually served on its own as a complete meal.

Preparation Time: 8 hours
Cooking Time: 1 hour, 30 minutes
Serving Size: 6

Ingredients:

Corn cobs (kernels removed)	5
Beans	2 ½ cups
Water	1 cup
Large onion (chopped)	1
Oil	1 tsp
Turmeric	1/2 tsp
Tomatoes (chopped)	2
Salt	1 tsp
Carrots (peeled, sliced)	3
Potatoes (peeled, cubed)	4
Coconut milk	1 ½ cups

Method:

1. Clean the beans and soak for 8 hours.
2. Wash the corn and beans. Place in a pot with water and cook for 1 hour.
3. In a pan, fry the onion until tender.
4. Add turmeric and stir for 2 minutes.
5. Add the chopped tomatoes and salt. Stir and cover. Cook on low heat for 3 minutes.
6. Add carrots, potatoes, coconut milk, corn and beans. Stir and cook on low heat for 15 minutes.
7. Serves well on its own.

12 - Kale Stretch
Sukuma Wiki

Description: *Sukuma wiki* is a nutritious and popular Kenyan side dish that can be made out of collards or kale. In Kenya, the plant traditionally used is a tall growing cabbage variety. Translated literally from Swahili, *sukuma wiki* means "to stretch out the week", implying that it is a staple used to stretch the family meals to last for the week. Often served with *ugali* and roasted meat or fish, *sukuma wiki* makes a typical Kenyan meal.

Preparation Time: 5 minutes
Cooking Time: 35 minutes
Serving Size: 6

Ingredients:

Oil	3 tbsp
Onion (finely chopped)	1
Kale or collard greens (chopped)	2 lbs
Tomatoes (chopped)	2 cups
Water	1 cup
Salt	to taste
Black pepper	to taste

Method:

1. Heat the oil over medium-high heat in a large, heavy-bottomed pot.
2. Add the onion and sauté until translucent.
3. Add the greens in batches. Sauté each addition until wilted.
4. Add the tomatoes, water, salt and pepper. Bring to a boil, then reduce heat to low and simmer gently for 20 minutes, until tender.
5. Adjust seasoning and serve with a little of the broth.

Variation:

1. Add a chopped chilli pepper or two with the onions if you like.
2. Add meat for more flavor. Kenyans would most likely use goat or beef.

13 - Beans in Coconut Sauce
M'baazi

Description: *M'Baazi* means "beans" in Swahili and is a traditional Kenyan vegetarian meal. It is often made from black-eyed peas in coconut milk, although any kind of beans may be used apart from green or waxed beans. *M'Baazi* can be eaten hot, but it is more tasteful when it is cooled. In Africa this dish is arranged traditionally on a green lettuce leaf, is decorated with parsley and tomato slices before serving.

Preparation Time: 5 minutes
Cooking Time: 1 hour, 10 minutes
Serving Size: 6

Ingredients:

Water	4 cups
Dried pea beans or other dried bean	1 cup
Vegetable oil or butter	4 tbsp
Bell pepper (finely chopped)	1/2 cup
Cayenne pepper	1/4 tsp
Onion (finely chopped)	1/2 cup
Salt	1 tsp
Coconut milk	1 cup
Lettuce	1/2 head
Tomato	1
Parsley	1/4 cup

Method:

1. Bring the salted water to a boil in a sauce pan. Cook the beans in it for 1 hour, until the beans have become tender.
2. Remove the beans from the heat and drain.
3. In another sauce pan, heat the oil or butter. Add the bell pepper, cayenne pepper, onion and salt. Sauté until the onion is tender but not browned.
4. Add the beans and continue to sauté until the onion is browned.
5. Add the coconut milk. Stir until the coconut milk reaches the consistency of a medium sauce.
6. Place in a bowl in the refrigerator until cold.
7. Serves well on lettuce leaves in a small dish. Place 1/2 cup of M'baazi in each dish and garnish with pieces of tomato and parsley.

14 - Spiced Kidney Beans
Maharagwe

Description: Although Kenyan, *maharagwe* is an example of the influence that Indian culture has had on some of the cuisine of East Africa. The turmeric, tomatoes and coconut milk are things you might find in any number of Indian dishes, but it all comes together with a distinctly East African feel. Typically *maharagwe* would be served with *ugali*.

Preparation Time: 5 minutes
Cooking Time: 20 minutes
Serving Size: 6

Ingredients:

Dried red kidney beans	1 cup
Medium yellow onions (chopped)	2
Oil	2 tbsp
Tomatoes (chopped)	3
Salt	1 tsp
Turmeric	2 tsp
Cayenne pepper	1 tsp
Garlic cloves (chopped)	3
Oregano	1 tsp
Coconut milk	2 cups

Method:

1. In a large pot, cover the beans with water and simmer until they are just tender.
2. Sauté onions in oil until golden brown.
3. Add the tomatoes, salt, turmeric, cayenne pepper, garlic, oregano and coconut milk to the pot and simmer several minutes until the beans are very tender and the tomatoes are cooked.
4. Serves well over *ugali* or rice.

15 - Yam Stew

Preparation Time: 5 minutes
Cooking Time: 20 minutes
Serving Size: 6

Ingredients:

Onions (sliced)	2
Oil	1 tbsp
Curry powder	1 tsp
Medium yam (peeled, cubed)	1
Carrots (peeled, cut in thin rounds)	4
Beans (cooked)	1 cup
Water	2 cups
Salt	1/2 tsp

Method:

1.Fry the onion in oil for 3 minutes.
2.Add curry powder and yam. Fry gently for 4 minutes.
3.Add carrots, beans, water and salt. Simmer for 10 minutes, until cooked.
4.Serves well with ugali, rice, mashed bananas or corn.

16 - Steak and Irio

Nyama Na Irio

Description: *Nyama na Irio* is a traditional Kenyan recipe for a classic dish of mashed potatoes blended with peas and sweet corn served with fried steak.

Preparation Time: 5 minutes
Cooking Time: 35 minutes
Serving Size: 6

Irio Ingredients:

Peas	2 cups
Corn	2 cups
Medium potatoes	5
Butter	3 tbsp
Salt	1 tsp
Black pepper	1/4 tsp

Irio Method:

1. Boil peas until cooked. Drain and mash.
2. Boil corn separately. Drain and set aside.
3. In a 2-quart saucepan, boil potatoes until cooked. Drain and mash. Add butter, salt and pepper.
4. Blend the mashed peas with the mashed potatoes until a smooth green color results.
5. Fold in the drained kernel corn.

Steak Ingredients:

Beef steak (cut into 1/2 inch strips)	3 lbs
Oil	1/2 cup
Flour	6 tbsp
Onion soup	2 cups
Salt	to taste
Black pepper	to taste
Tabasco	to taste
Irio (see recipe)	6 cups

Steak Method:

1. In a large skillet, sauté beef strips in oil, until lightly browned.
2. Remove the steak from the skillet and blend in flour.
3. Add onion soup and cook to medium-sauce consistency.
4. Correct the seasoning with salt, pepper and tabasco.
5. Return the steak to the sauce.
6. To serve, place about 1 cup of Irio in the center of each dinner plate. Form a hole in the center about 2 inches in diameter. Fill the hole with 1/2 cup of the sautéed steak and gravy.

17 - Roasted Meat

Nyama Choma

Description: *Nyama Choma* means roasted meat in Swahili and for many it is the ultimate Kenyan experience. Visitors are often amazed by the amount of *nyama choma* that Kenyans consume. This recipe for *nyama choma* features an innovative use of curry powder in a marinade. Turmeric, paprika and coriander are optional spices as those are not typical ingredients in the average Kenyan family, but will certainly add flavor in the *nyama choma*. This recipe works well with any red meat, however beef short ribs are the favorite of many Kenyans.

Preparation Time: 2 hours, 5 minutes
Cooking Time: 15 minutes
Serving Size: 6

Ingredients:

Lemons (juiced)	2
Garlic cloves (minced)	2
Curry powder	3 tsp
Turmeric	2 tsp
Coriander	1 tsp
Paprika	2 tsp
Salt	1 tsp
Black pepper	1 tsp
Beef short ribs	2 lbs

Method:

1. Combine the lemon juice, garlic, curry powder, turmeric, coriander, paprika, salt and pepper in a large glass dish. Mix well.
2. Add meat. Stir to cover the meat with marinade. Allow to marinate for 2 hours.
3. Grill the meat over charcoal or broil in a hot oven.
4. Serves well with Irio or Ugali.

18 - Chicken Curry

Preparation Time: 5 minutes
Cooking Time: 1 hour, 10 minutes
Serving Size: 4

Ingredients:

Chicken (skinned, cut into pieces)	4 lbs
Salt	to taste
Ground white pepper	to taste
Garlic cloves (minced)	4
Medium onion (finely chopped)	1
Vegetable oil	2 tbsp
Tomatoes (skinned, chopped)	6
Garam masala	a pinch
Coriander (ground)	a pinch
Black pepper	1/2 tsp
Nutmeg	1/2 tsp
Turmeric	1/2 tsp
Ground ginger	1/2 tsp
Cayenne pepper	1/2 tsp
Cumin	1/2 tsp
Water	3 cups

Method:

1. Pre-heat oven to 350°F.
2. Rub the salt, pepper and garlic into the chicken pieces and roast them in the oven for 40 minutes, until golden brown.
3. Cook the onions in the oil over high heat until crisp. Remove the onions from the saucepan and mash them.
4. Add the tomatoes, spices and water to saucepan and cook 5 minutes, until thick.
5. Add the chicken pieces, garlic and the mashed onions. Simmer all for 20 minutes, until cooked through.
6. Serves well with rice.

19 - Chicken and Rice

Biriani

Description: *Biriani* is a dish that originated from the Kenya coast. It is a highly nutritious and delicious meal that is a basic staple of Kenya Coast people. Making *Biriani* is a process that dates back thousands of years and many variations exist within regions of Kenya. Omit the potatoes for optimal authenticity.

Preparation Time: 5 minutes
Cooking Time: 1 hour
Serving Size: 6

Ingredients:

Beef, goat or chicken (cut into pieces)	2 lbs
Rice	2 cups
Onions	2 cups
Potatoes (peeled, sliced)	2 cups
Medium papaya (de-seeded, grated)	1
Sour milk or plain yogurt	1 ½ cups
Limes (juiced)	2
Tomatoes	1/2 cup
Garlic clove (minced)	1
Fresh ginger (minced)	1 piece
Cardamom pods	5
Cloves	5
Cinnamon sticks	2
Cumin seeds	1 tsp
Coriander seeds	1 tsp
Whole black peppercorns	1 tsp
Oil	
Tomato paste	1 cup

Method:

1. Place meat into a heavy saucepan with the papaya, garlic and ginger. Add the sour milk or yogurt and the lime juice. Set over a low heat and stir every few minutes for 30 minutes.
2. While this is cooking, grind all the spices together and set aside.
3. Slice the onions and fry in oil until brown and crisp. Remove from the fat.
4. Fry the potatoes in oil until golden brown. Remove and set aside apart from the onions.
5. Add the spices to the meat and the skinned tomatoes together with 5 tbsp of oil. Mix together well, then add the tomato paste. Continue cooking over low heat for 15 minutes until the meat is really tender and the sauce thick and creamy.
6. Add 1/4 cup of water and cook for 20 minutes to make sure all the flavours have blended together.
7. Prepare and cook the rice.
8. To serve, place a layer of rice on the dish. Pour over the meat mixture and top with the fried onions. Place the sliced potatoes on the side.

20 - Kenyan Chicken

Ingoho

Description: *Ingoho* is chicken cooked by the Luhya tribe of Kenya. It is their signature meal, which they serve to important visitors.

Preparation Time: 5 minutes
Cooking Time: 1 hour, 35 minutes
Serving Size: 6

Ingredients:

Whole chicken	1
Large onion (chopped)	1
Garlic clove (minced)	1
Salt	to taste
Large tomatoes (sliced)	2
Cooking oil	
Medium green chilli	1
Coriander	1 bunch

Method:

1. Roast the chicken and cut it into medium sized pieces.
2. Boil the chicken for 1 hour to make it tender. Strain the broth but keep it aside. Do not throw it away.
3. Shallow fry the chopped onions.
4. Add the garlic and salt. Stir.
5. Add sliced tomatoes and cook for about 10 minutes. Stir to make a paste.
6. Add the chicken as well as the chopped chilli and coriander. Stir and simmer for 10 minutes.
7. Add a small amount of the chicken broth that was set aside and mix well.
8. Add any spices of your choice and simmer for 5 minutes.
9. Serves well with rice, ugali, steamed cabbage, sukuma wiki, irio, chapati, pilau or vegetables on the side.

21 - Chicken in Coconut Sauce

Kuku Paka

Description: This simple dish, sometimes called *kuku na nazi*, is a fabulous coconut curry from the East African coast. It is a perfect illustration of how African, Arab and Indian influences join in the coastal region.

Preparation Time: 5 minutes
Cooking Time: 1 hour
Serving Size: 6

Ingredients:

Onion (chopped)	1
Hot chilli peppers (chopped)	3
Ginger (peeled, chopped)	2 tbsp
Garlic clove	2
Oil	1/4 cup
Curry powder	1 tbsp
Cumin	2 tsp
Chopped tomatoes or tomato sauce	2 cups
Chicken (cut into pieces)	3 lbs
Coconut milk	2 cups
Salt	to taste
Black pepper	to taste
Cilantro (chopped)	1/2 cup

Method:

1. Add the onion, chilli peppers, ginger and garlic to a food processor or blender and process until smooth. Add a little water if necessary.
2. Heat the oil in a large pot over medium heat. Add the onion puree, curry powder and cumin. Sauté, stirring frequently for 5 minutes, until cooked down.
3. Stir in the tomatoes and simmer for 4 minutes.
4. Add the chicken, coconut milk, salt and pepper. Reduce heat to low and simmer covered for 45 minutes, until the chicken is cooked through and tender. Add more water as needed.
5. Stir in the cilantro, adjust seasoning with salt and pepper.
6. Serves well with rice or chapati.

Variation:

1. For more authentic flavor, grill the chicken pieces before stirring them into the simmering sauce.
2. Some recipes add potatoes to the curry. The potatoes can be cooked ahead, cut into chunks and stirred into the curry toward the end.

22 - Green Beans and Potato Curry

Posho Bateta Nu Shak

Preparation Time: 5 minutes
Cooking Time: 20 minutes
Serving Size: 4

Ingredients:

Medium potatoes (washed, cubed)	2 cups
Kenyan beans (chopped)	2 cups
Mustard seeds	1 tsp
Oil	1 tbsp
Salt	1 tsp
Turmeric	1 tsp
Chilli powder	1 tsp
Cumin	1 tsp
Garlic cloves (minced)	3
Brown sugar	1 tsp
Canned tomatoes	1/2 cup
Lemon juice	2 tsp
Coriander	1 bunch

Method:

1. Cook the potatoes in boiling water.
2. Soak the beans in cold water.
3. Heat the oil in a saucepan over medium heat. Add the mustard seeds.
4. When seeds start popping, add the cooked potatoes and the soaked beans to the saucepan.
5. Add the salt, turmeric, chilli powder, cumin, garlic and sugar. Stir well and cook over low heat for 3 minutes.
6. Add 1/2 cup of water and cook for 5 minutes.
7. Add the tomatoes and lemon juice, and cook for 5 minutes.
8. Serves well sprinkled with fresh coriander and accompanied by hot chapatis.

23 - Chickpea Curry

Preparation Time: 5 minutes
Cooking Time: 20 minutes
Serving Size: 6

Ingredients:

Vegetable oil	1 tbsp
Cumin seeds	1/4 tsp
Turmeric	1/2 tsp
Medium onion (chopped)	1
Garlic cloves (finely chopped)	2
Ginger (finely chopped)	1 piece
Tomatoes (chopped)	2
Chickpea (soaked, cooked until tender)	1/2 cup
Cayenne pepper	1/2 tsp
Salt	to taste
Lemon juice	1 tsp

Method:
1. Heat the oil and add cumin seeds and turmeric.
2. When seeds begin to pop add the onion, garlic and ginger.
3. Once the onions are translucent, add tomatoes.
4. Add cooked chickpeas and heat the mixture carefully trying not to mash the beans.
5. Add cayenne pepper and salt. Sprinkle with lemon juice.

24 - Baked Curried Fish

Mtuza Wa Samaki

Description: *Mtuza wa Samaki* is a traditional Kenyan recipe for a classic fish and onion curry. The fish is enveloped with a peppery sauce. Often fresh fish is eaten without bones being removed in Kenya.

Preparation Time: 10 minutes
Cooking Time: 45 minutes
Serving Size: 6

Ingredients:

White fish	2 lbs
Oil	2 tbsp
Large yellow onions (sliced)	3
Cayenne pepper (optional)	1 tsp
Garlic cloves	3
Tomato paste	1/2 cup
White vinegar	1/2 cup
Ground cardamom	1/2 tsp
Cumin (optional)	1/2 tsp
Salt	1/2 tsp

Method:

1. Preheat oven to 350ºF.
2. Lay the fish in a baking pan.
3. Heat the oil to a moderate temperature and fry the onion slices until they are translucent.
4. Arrange onions over the fish.
5. Combine the remaining ingredients in a blender or food processor until smooth.
6. Pour mixture over fish, cover the pot and simmer for 40 minutes until fish is just cooked.

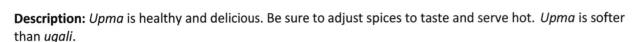

25 - Semonilla and Vegetables

Upma

Description: *Upma* is healthy and delicious. Be sure to adjust spices to taste and serve hot. *Upma* is softer than *ugali*.

Preparation Time: 5 minutes
Cooking Time: 15 minutes
Serving Size: 6

Ingredients:

Butter	2 tbsp
Cumin seeds	1 tsp
Turmeric	1/2 tsp
Bay leaf	1
Onion (finely chopped)	1
Cashews (chopped)	5
Garlic cloves (finely chopped)	2
Semolina, farina or cream of wheat	1/2 cup
Carrot (finely chopped)	1
Peas	1/2 cup
Water	1 cup
Cayenne pepper	1/2 tsp

Method:

1.Melt butter and mix together the spices (except for cayenne pepper), onion, cashews and garlic. Sauté until lightly browned.

2.Add semolina and continue to sauté over low heat for 5 minutes stirring constantly.

3.Add carrots, peas and the water. Add more water if necessary and continue stirring for 3 minutes until the semolina is cooked. Most of the water should get absorbed.

4.Add cayenne pepper and serve hot.

26 - Little Fried Snacks
Maandazi

Description: *Maandazi* are East African doughnuts and a popular treat in the Swahili areas of Kenya. You can find these delicious donuts in large urban areas and also among the Swahili people of East Africa. Most small restaurants, called *hotelis* in Kenya, serve *mandazi*. You can also find *mandazi* being sold by street vendors. *Maandazi* is often prepared with oil, as butter is a luxury ingredient in Kenya. Cardamom seeds are optional. They can be seen in triangular, rectangular and square shapes.

Preparation Time: 20 minutes
Cooking Time: 10 minutes
Serving Size: 2 bowls

Ingredients:

Butter	1 cup
Sugar	5 tbsp
Large eggs (beaten)	2
Milk	1/2 cup
Cardamom seeds (ground)	6
Baking powder	2 tsp
All purpose wheat flour	4 ½ cups
Water	1/2 cup
Vegetable oil	6 cups
Powdered sugar	

Method:

1. Mix and whisk together the butter and sugar.
2. Add the eggs and milk. Mix.
3. Add the ground cardamom and baking powder, then add the flour and water. If the dough is sticky, add more flour. Knead well until the dough is smooth and soft.
4. Cut the dough into 3 balls and roll out each to about 12-15 inches in diameter and 1/4 inch thick.
5. Slice into 2-inch strips and cut into squares.
6. Heat the oil in a deep frying pan. To test if the oil is hot enough, drop in one mandaazi. If it sinks then floats to the top, the oil is ready.
7. Cook the maandazi a few pieces at a time in the pan. Turn pieces often until they are golden brown. Remove from the pan, drain and cool.
8. Serves well sprinkled with powdered sugar, alongside a coffee or chai.

27 - Crunchy Bananas
N'dizi

Description: *N'dizi* are baked bananas which are first steamed, then covered in roasted peanuts. They can be served as a snack or dessert.

Preparation Time: 5 minutes
Cooking Time: 15 minutes
Serving Size: 6

Ingredients:

Bananas (peeled, sliced into rounds)	6
Water	1 tbsp
Unsalted butter (melted)	4 tbsp
Unsalted peanuts (chopped)	3/4 cup

Method:

1. Preheat oven to 400ºF.
2. Warm a skillet over medium-high heat. Add the banana rounds and water to the skillet, cover and let steam for 1 minute. Drain the liquid.
3. Dip the banana rounds in melted butter and then coat with chopped nuts and set on a baking tray.
4. Bake for 4 minutes, then flip the rounds and bake for 6 minutes, until the peanuts are roasted.

28 - Tropical Fruit

Description: In Kenya, fruit is usually eaten for dessert in place of sweets. Kenya has a wide variety of tropical fruits including bananas, mangoes, pineapples, papayas, guavas, matoke, passion fruit, pears and seasonal citrus fruits.

Preparation Time: 5 minutes
Serving Size: 6

Ingredients:

Passion fruit	4
Pawpaw (peeled, seeded, cubed)	1
Bananas (peeled, sliced)	2
Mango (peeled, seeded, cubed)	1
Lemon (juice)	1/2

Method:

1.Scoop the passion fruit into a large bowl.
2.Add the pawpaw, bananas and mango. Toss together gently.
3.Pour the lemon and toss again.
4.Serve in small fruit bowls.

Printed in Great Britain
by Amazon.co.uk, Ltd.,
Marston Gate.